THE PHILOSOPHY
OF THE
VEDANTA

THE PHILOSOPHY
OF THE
VEDANTA

BY

PAUL DEUSSEN

AND

THE VEDANTASARA
OF
SADANANDA YOGENDRA

TRANSLATED WITH ANNOTATIONS

BY

G. A. JACOB

GYAN

Published by

Gyan Publishing House
5, Ansari Road
Daryaganj, New Delhi-110002
Phone: 011-47034999, 9811692060
E-mail: books@gyanbooks.com

Distribution Network
gyanbooks.com
India, USA, Canada, UK, Australia, France

ISBN : 978-81-212-2780-3 (HB)
First Published, 1957

2nd Impression 2021

Printed at: Gyan Press, Delhi.

The Philosophy of the Vedanta
Translated By: G. A. Jacob

THE PHILOSOPHY OF THE VEDANTA

BY

PAUL DEUSSEN

AND

THE VEDANTASARA

OF

SADANANDA YOGENDRA

TRANSLATED WITH ANNOTATIONS

BY

G. A. JACOB

SUSIL GUPTA (INDIA) LIMITED
CALCUTTA 12
1957

PUBLISHERS' NOTE

THE first two papers by Deussen, published in this volume, appeared in the *Indian Antiquary,* 1902, and was reprinted in 1907 in a little volume entitled "Outlines of Indian Philosophy" with an appendix on the Philosophy of the Vedanta in its relations to occidental metaphysics. The paper "On the Philosophy of the Vedanta" was originally an address delivered before the Bombay Branch of the Royal Asiatic Society in February, 1893.

The concluding treatise, the Vedantasara of Sadananda Yogendra, translated with annotations by G. A. Jacob, was first published in 1881 in the Trubner's Oriental Series as A Manual of Hindu Pantheism.

The text of the Vedantasara which the author used is that published in Calcutta in 1875 by Pandit Jivananda Vidyasagar, with the Commentary of Nrisinhasaraswati.

PAUL DEUSSEN

1845 -

BORN Jan. 7, 1845, at Oberdreis near Coblenz: son of Adam Deussen, pastor; educated at Schulpforta near Naumburg: studied at Bonn, Tubingen and Berlin: Sanskrit under Lassen and Gildemeister, classical philology, theology: Phil. Dr. at Marburg, 1869: teacher at the Gymnasiums at Minden and Marburg, 1869-72, and tutor in Russian families at Geneva, Aix-la-Chapelle, and Terny in Russia, 1872-80: taught philosophy (the subject to which he was chiefly devoted) and Sanskrit, as Privat-docent at the University of Geneva: and philosophy at the Polytechnical School at Aix-la-Chapelle, 1875-9. While at Geneva, his resolution was made to devote his life to the study of Indian philosophy (1873). Since his return from Russia and residence in Berlin, from 1881 to 1889, this has been his main work: taught philosophy at Berlin University, first as Privat-docent then as Professor: since 1889, Ordinary Professor of Philosophy at the University of Kiel; has travelled much in various parts of the world: over the greater part of India, 1892-3. In 1904, the Order of the Red Eagle, 4th Class, was conferred upon him. Among his chief works may be mentioned: *Das System des Vedanta*, 1883: *Die Sutras des Vedanta*, 1887: *On the Philosophy of the Vedanta in its relations to Occidental Metaphysics*, Bombay, 1893; *Sechzig Upanishads des Veda*, 1897: *Geschichte der Philosophie* (I and II on the Vedic Hymns and Upanishads: III-VI in preparation), 1894, 1899: "Outlines of Indian Philosophy," in the *Indian Antiquary*, 1902: *Erinnerungen an Indian*, 1904.

CONTENTS

I. OUTLINES OF INDIAN PHILOSOPHY

II. ON THE PHILOSOPHY OF THE VEDANTA

III. THE VEDANTASARA

THE PHILOSOPHY OF THE VEDANTA

IMPORTANCE OF INDIAN PHILOSOPHY

Among the pretexts by which European idleness tries to escape the study of Indian philosophy we hear most frequently the remark that the philosophy of the Indians is quite different from our own and has nothing whatever to do with the development of Occidental religion and philosophy. The fact is perfectly true; but far from being a reason for neglecting the study of Indian wisdom, it furnishes us with the strongest argument in favour of devoting ourselves to it all the more. The philosophy of the Indians must become for every one who takes any interest in the investigation of philosophical truth, an object of the highest interest; for Indian philosophy is and will be the only possible parallel to what so far the Europeans have considered as philosophy. In fact, modern European philosophy has sprung from the scholasticism of the Middle Ages; medieval thought again is a product of Greek philosophy on the one hand and of the Biblical dogma on the other. The doctrine of the Bible has again its roots in part in the oldest Semitic creed and in part in the Persian religion of Zoroaster, which, as an intermediate link between the Old and the New Testament, has exercised more influence than is commonly attributed to it. In this way the whole of European thought from Pythagoras and Xenophanes, from Moses and Zoroaster, through Platonism and Christianity down to the Kantian and post-Kantian philosophy, forms a complex of ideas, whose elements are variously related to and dependent on each other. On the other hand Indian philosophy through all the centuries of its development has taken its course uninfluenced by West-Asiatic and European thought; and precisely for this reason the comparison of European philosophy with that of the Indians is of the highest interest. Where both agree the presumption is that their conclusions are correct, no less than in a case where two calculators working by different methods arrive at the same result; and where Indian and European views differ it is an open question on which side the truth is probably to be found.

PERIODS OF INDIAN PHILOSOPHY

2. Indian philosophy falls naturally into three periods; these three periods are equally strongly marked in the general history of Indian civilisation and are dependent on the geography of India. India, as Sir William Jones has already remarked, has

the form of a square whose four angles are turned to the four cardinal points, and are marked by the Hindu Kush in the north, Cape Comorin in the south, and the mouths of the Ganges and Indus in the east and west. If a line be drawn from the mouth of the Indus to that of the Ganges (nearly coinciding with the tropic of Cancer), the square is divided into two triangles — Hindusthan in the north, and the Dekhan in the south. If again in the northern triangle we let fall a perpendicular from the vertex upon the base, this divides northern India into the valley of the Indus and the plain of the Ganges, separated by the desert of Marusthala. Thus India falls into three parts—(1) the Punjab, (2) the plain of the Ganges, (3) the Dekhan plateau. To these three geographical divisions correspend the three periods of Indian life:—(1) The domain of the Aryan Hindus in the oldest period was limited to the valley of the Indus with its five tributaries; the only literary monuments of this epoch are the 1017 hymns of the Rigveda. Though chiefly serving religious purposes they give by the way a lively and picturesque delineation of that primitive manner of life in which there were no castes, no *acramas* (stages of life), and no Brahmanical order of life in general. The hymns of the Rigveda display not only the ancient Indian polytheism in its full extent, but contain also in certain of the later hymns the first germs of a philosophical view of the world. (2) It may have been about 1000 B.C. that the Aryans starting from the Punjab began to extend their conquests to the east and occupied little by little the plain extending from the Himalayas in the north and the Vindhyas in the south to the mouth of the Ganges. The conquest of this territory may have been accomplished, roughly speaking, between 1000 and 500 B.C. As literary monuments of this second period of Indian life we find the *Samhitas* of the *Yajur-*, *Sama-*, and *Atharvaveda*, together with the Brahmanas and their culmination in the Upanishads. Hand in hand with this literary development we have under the spiritual dominion of the Brahmans the establishment of that original organisation which as the Brahmanical order of life has survived in India with some modification until the present day. (3) After these two periods, which we may distinguish as "old-Vedic" and "new-Vedic", follows a third period of Indian history—the "post-Vedic"—beginning about 50 B.C. with the rise of the heretical tendencies of Buddhism and Jainism, and producing in the succeeding centuries a large number of literary works in which, together with poetry, grammar, law, medicine and astronomy, a rich collection of philosophical works in Sanskrit permits us to trace the development of the philosophical mind down to the present time. In this period India, *i.e.*, Brahmanical, civilisation makes its way round the coast of Southern India and Ceylon and penetrates conquering into the remotest districts of Central India.

FIRST PERIOD

PHILOSOPHY OF THE RIGVEDA

3. The oldest interpretation of Nature and therefore the first philosophy of a people is its religion, and for the origin and essence of religion there is no book in the world more instructive than the Rigveda; Homer in Greece, and the most ancient parts of the Old Testament show religion in an advanced state of development which presupposes many preliminary stages now lost to us. In India alone we can trace back religion to its first origin. It is true that the hymns of the Rigveda also show religion in a later stage of development; some primitive gods stand already in the background, as Dyaus (heaven) and Prithivi (earth); they are rarely mentioned but with an awe which shows their high position at an earlier period. Another god, Varuna (the starry heaven), is still prominent, but even he is in danger of being superseded by Indra, the god of the thunderstorm and of war; and a remarkable hymn (iv. 42) exhibits a dialogue between Varuna and Indra, in which each boasts his greatness, while the poet notwithstanding the full respect for Varuna, betrays a certain partiality for Indra. This case and many others show that the Rigvedic religion also is in an advanced state of development; but the names of the gods considered etymologically and the character of the myths related of them, are so transparent that we are able in nearly every case to discover the original meaning of the god in question. Thus there can be no doubt that Varuna[1] is a personification of the heaven with its regular daily revolution, and that he only in later times became a god of the waters. Other gods represent the sun in its various aspects: Surya the radiant globe of the sun, Savitar the arouser, Vishnu the vivifying force, Mitra the benevolent light, the friend of mankind, and Pushan, the shepherd of the world. Besides these we have the two Asvins, a divine pair who bring help in time of need, and seem to mean originally the twilight with which the day begins and the terrors of the night have an end. A very transparent personification of the dawn is Ushas (Aurora)[2] represented as a beautiful maiden displaying every morning her charm before the eyes of the world. If from

1 Gk. *Ouranos*. 2 Gk. *Eos*.

these gods of the luminous heaven we pass to the second part of the universe, the atmosphere, we meet here among others Vayu or Vata, god of the winds, Parjanya, the rain-god, the terrible Rudra, who probably personifies the destructive and purifying lightning, further the Maruts, the merry gods of the storm and above all Indra, the god of the thunderstorm, who in his battles against the demons that hinder the rain from falling, is the typical god of warfare and thus the ideal of the Hindu of the heroic epoch. Lastly, coming to the earth, there are many phenomena of Nature and life considered as divine powers, but above all Agni, god of the destructive and helpful fire, and a Soma, a personification of the intoxicating power of the soma-drink, which inspires gods and men to heroic deeds. This short sketch shows clearly what the gods were in ancient India and what *mutatis mutandis* they are originally in every religion of the world, namely, personifications of natural forces and natural phenomena. Man in passing from the brute state to human consciousness found himself surrounded by and dependent on various natural powers: the nourishing earth, the fertilising heaven, the wind, the rain, the thunderstorm, etc., and ascribed to them not only will, like that of man, which was perfectly correct, but also human personality, human desires and human weaknesses, which certainly was wrong. These personified natural powers were further considered as the origin, the maintainers and controllers of what man found in himself as the moral law, opposed to the egoistic tendencies natural to man. Thus the religion of the Rigveda may teach us that gods, wherever we meet them in the world, are compounded of two elements—a mythological, so far as they are personifications of natural powers and phenomena, and a moral element so far as these personifications are considered as the authors and guardians of the moral law. Let us add that the better religion is that in which the moral element preponderates, and the less perfect religion that in which the mythological element is developed at the cost of the moral. If we apply this criterion to the religion of the Rigveda, we must recognize that, notwithstanding its high interest in so many respects, it cannot as a religion claim a specially high position; for the Rigvedic gods, though at the same time the guardians of morality (*gopa ritasya*), are mainly regarded as being of superhuman powers but egotistic tendencies. This moral deficiency of the Rigvedic religion has certainly been the chief cause of the surprisingly rapid decay of the old-Vedic worship; this decay and at the same time the first germs of philosophical thought we can trace in certain of the later hymns of the Rigveda, as we shall now proceed to demonstrate.

DECAY OF THE OLD-VEDIC RELIGION

4. In certain later hymns of the Rigveda there are unmistakeable signs that the ancient creed was falling into disrepute. A beautiful hymn (x. 117) recommends the duty of benevolence without any reference to the gods, apparently because they were too weak a support for pure moral actions. Another hymn (x. 151) is addressed not to a god but to Faith, and praising the merit of faith, concludes with the prayer: "O Faith, make us faithful." In a time of unshaken faith such a prayer would hardly have been offered. But we have clearer proofs that the old-Vedic faith began to fade. In a hymn (ii. 12) to Indra, the principal god of the Vedic Hindu, the poet says:—"the terrible god, whose existence they doubt, and ask 'where is he', nay, whom they deny, saying, 'he is not', this god will destroy his enemies like play-things"—and doubts like this occur now and then; but even more frequently we meet passages and entire hymns which evidently ridicule the gods and their worship, more especially that of the god Indra. Everybody in the world, says the hymn ix. 112, pursues his egoistic interests, the joiner hopes for broken wheels, the doctor for broken limbs, the blacksmith looks for customers; I am a poet, says the author, my father is a physician, my mother turns the mill in the kitchen, and so we all persue our own advantage, as a herdsman his cows. This little piece of humorous poetry would be perfectly innocent were it not that after each verse comes the refrain, probably taken from an old hymn: "Thou, O Soma, flow for Indra", which evidently means that Indra also seeks his own advantage and is an egotist like other people.

Even more bold is the scorn in hymn x. 119, which introduces Indra in the merriest humour, ready to give away everything, ready to destroy the earth and all that it contains, boasting of his greatness in ridiculous fashion,—all this because, as the refrain tells us, he is in an advanced stage of intoxication, caused by excessive appreciation of the soma offered to him. Another hymn (vii. 103) sings of the frogs, comparing their voices to the noise of a Brahmanical school and their hopping round the tank to the behaviour of drunken priests celebrating a nocturnal offering of Soma. As here the holy teachers and the priests, so in another hymn (x. 82) the religious poetry of the Veda and its authors are depreciated by the words: "The Vedic minstrels, wrapped in fog and floods of words, go on the stump to make a livelihood."

5. The age in which such words were possible was certainly ripe for philosophy; and accordingly we see emerging in certain later hymns of the Rigveda the thought by which here as well as in Greece philosophy begins—the conception of the unity of the world. Just as Xenophanes in Greece puts above all the popular gods his one deity who is nothing more than the universe considered as a unity, we find in the Rigveda a remarkable seeking and enquiring after that one from which, as an eternal, unfathomable, unspeakable unity, all gods, worlds, and creatures originate. The Hindus arrive at this Monism by a method essentially different from that of other countries. Monotheism was attained in Egypt by a mechanical identification of the various local gods, in Palestine by proscription of other gods and violent persecution of their worshippers for the benefit of the nationanl god, Jehovah. In India they reached Monism though not Monotheism on a more philosophical path, seeing through the veil of the manifold the unity which underlies it. Thus the profound and difficult hymn, i. 164, pointing out the difference of the names Agni, Indra and Vayu, comes to the bold conclusion: "there is one being of which the poets of the hymns speak under various names." The same idea of the unity of the universe is expressed in the wonderful hymn x. 129, which as the most remarkable monument of the oldest philosophy we here translate:

1. In the beginning there was neither Non-Being nor Being, neither atmosphere nor sky beyond—What enveloped all things? Where were they, in whose care? What was the ocean, the unfathomable depth?

2. At that time there was neither mortal nor immortal, neither night nor day.—That being the only one, breathed without air in independence. Beyond it nought existed.

3. Darkness was there; by darkness enshrouded in the beginning, an ocean without lights was all this world;—but the pregnant germ which was enveloped by the husk was born by the strength of penitence.

4. And forth went as the first-born Kama (love) which was the primordial seed of mind.—Thus wise men meditating have found out the link of Non-Being and Being in the heart.

5. They threw their plumbline across the universe. What was then below and what above? There were seedbearers; there was mighty striving; independence beneath, exertion above.

6. But who knows and who can tell from where was born, from where came forth creation?—The gods came afterwards into existence. Who then can say from whence creation came?

7. He from whom this creation proceeded, whether he created it or not, He whose eye watches it in the highest heaven, He perhaps knows it—or perhaps he knows it not.

I add a metrical translation[1]:

1. Non-Being was not, Being was not yet;
 There was no vault of heaven, no realm of air,
 Where was the ocean, where the deep abyss?
 What mantled all? Where was it, in whose care?
2. Death was not known nor yet immortal life;
 Night was not born and day was not yet seen.
 Airless he breathed in primevality
 The One beyond whom nought hath ever been.
3. Darkness prevailed at first, a chaos dread;
 'Twas this great world, clad in its cloak of night.
 And then was brought to being the germ of all,
 The One pent in this husk, by *Tapas'* might.
4. And first of all from him proceeded love,
 Kama, the primal seed and germ of thought.
 In Non-existence was by sages found
 Existence' root, when in the heart they sought.
5. When through the realm of Being their arc they spanned,
 What was beneath it, what was in their ken?
 Germ-carriers beneath? Strivings above!
 The seeds of things were hid, the things were seen.
6. Whence sprang the universe? Who gave it form?
 What eye hath seen its birth? Its source who knows?
 Before the world was made the gods were not;
 Who then shall tell us whence these things arose?
7. He who hath moulded and called forth the world,
 Whether he hath created it or not,
 Who gazeth down on it from heaven's heights,
 He knoweth it; or doth he know it not?

ATTEMPTS TO DETERMINE THAT UNITY

6. The great thought of the unity of all things having been conceived, the next task was to find out what this unity was. For the attempt to determine it the hymn x. 121, is especially typical which, starting apparently from the hymn x. 129, or a similar piece of work, seeks a name for that unknown god who was the last unity of the universe. In the first eight verses the poet points out the wonders of creation and concludes each

1 I am indebted for this translation to N. W. Thomas.

verse by asking "Who is that god, that we may worship him? In the ninth verse he finds a name for that new and unknown deity, calling it Prajapati (lord of the creatures). This name in striking contrast to the names of the old Vedic gods, is evidently not of popular origin but the creation of a philosophical thinker. Henceforth Prajapati occupies the highest position in the pantheon, until he is displaced by two other, more philosophical conceptions—Brahman and Atman. These three names, Prajapati, Brahman and Atman dominate the whole philosophical development from the Rigdeva to the Upanishads. The oldest term Prajapati is merely mythological and the transition from it to the term Atman (which, as we shall see, is highly philosophical) is very natural. But it is very characteristic of the Hindu mind that this transition is accomplished by means of an intermediate term Brahman, which was originally merely ritual in its meaning and application, signifying "prayer". At the time of the Upanishads the name Prajapati is nearly forgotten and appears only now and then as a mythological figure; while the terms Brahman and Atman have become identical and serve in turn to express that being which, as we shall see, is the only object of which the Upanishads treat. We have now to trace the history of these three terms in detail.

HISTORY OF PRAJAPATI

7. It is characteristic of the way in which Indian religion developed that a mere philosophical abstraction such as Prajapati might put in the background all the other gods and occupy in the time of the Brahmanas the highest place in the Hindu pantheon. Prajapati in this period is considered as the father of gods, men and demons, as the creator and ruler of the world. Numerous passages of the *Brahmanas,* intended to recommend some ritual usage, describe the rite or formula as produced by Prajapati and employed by him in the creation of the world. Such passages regularly begin with the phrase that in the beginning Prajapati alone was, that he performed penance and thereby worthily prepared himself for creating the different gods, the worlds and the various implements and materials of sacrifice. All the gods depend on him; in him they take refuge when harassed by the demons; and to him as arbitrator they come if some quarrel about their relative dignity arises. Into these details we will not enter; we will here only point out that the Indian idea of creation is essentially different from that current in the Christian world. Prajapati does not create a world; he transforms himself, his body and his limbs into the different

parts of the universe. Therefore in creating he is swallowed up, he falls to pieces, and is restored by the performance of some rite which is in this way recommended. In later texts we observe a tendency to get rid of Prajapati whether by deriving him from a still higher principle, such as the primordial waters, the Non-ent preceding his existence, or by explaining him away and identifying him with the creating mind, the creating word, the sacrifice or the year as principles of the world. In older passages Prajapati creates, among other ritual objects, the Brahman; later passages on the other hand make him dependent on the Brahman.

HISTORY OF THE BRAHMAN

8. Every attempt to explain this central idea of Indian philosophy must proceed from the fact that the word Brahman throughout the Rigveda in which it occurs more than 200 times, signifies without exception nothing more than "prayer". Like Soma and other gifts, the prayer of the poet is offered to the gods; they enjoy it; they are fortified by it for their heroic deeds; and as man stands in need of the various benefits of the gods, the gods need for their welfare the offerings and especially the prayers of mankind; "prayer is a 'tonic' of the gods"; "Indra for his battles is fortified by prayer" (offered to him); phrases like these occur frequently in the Rigveda; thus the idea became more and more prominent that human prayer is a power which surpasses in potency even the might of the gods. In the moments of religious devotion man felt himself raised above his own individuality, felt awakening in himself that metaphysical power on which all worlds with their gods and creatures are dependent. By this curious development[1] Brahman, the old name for prayer, became the most usual name for the creative principle of the world. An old Rigvedic question "which was the tree, which was the wood, of which they hewed the earth and heaven"? is repeated in a *Brahmana* text, and followed by the answer: "The Brahman was the tree, the wood from which they hewed the earth and heaven." Here the term Brahman has become already what it has been through all the following centuries—the most common name for eternal and changeless principle of the world.

HISTORY OF THE ATMAN

9. A better name even than Brahman, and perhaps the best name which philosophy has found in any language to designate the principle of the world, is the word Atman, which properly is the exact equivalent of the english "Self". Thus Atman

1 Comparable to the history of the Biblical *Logos*.

means that which remains if we take away from our person all that is Non-self, foreign, all that comes and passes away; it means "the changeless, inseparable essence of our own Self", and on the other hand the essence of the Self of the whole world. It is not possible, as in the case of Prajapati and Brahman, to frame a history of the word Atman. It has no regular development but we see it emerge here and there in proportion as the thinker seeks and finds a more clear-out expression for the word Brahman to name that being which can never by any means be taken away from us, and therefore forms the only true essence of our nature, our *atman*, out Self. With this word we have reached the sphere of the Upanishads; we must now say a few words on these most remarkable monuments of ancient Indian literature.

SECOND PERIOD

PHILOSOPHY OF THE UPANISHADS

10. If we compare the Veda and the Bible we may say that the Old Testament is represented in the Veda by all the hymns and *Brahmana* texts, which serve the purpose of ritual worship. But, as the Old Testament is superseded by the New, so in the Veda all ritual performances with their rewards are declared insufficient and replaced by a higher view of things in those wonderful texts which, forming as a rule the concluding chapters of each Veda, are called Vedanta (end of the Veda) or Upanishads (confidential sitting, secred doctrine). The four Vedas produced different branches or schools, each of which has handed down the common content of the Vedas in a slightly different form. Thus every Vedic school had, besides the Samhita or collection of verses and formulas, a special Brahmanam as its ritual text-book, and a longer or shorter Upanishad, which forms its dogmatic text-book. Therefore all the Upanishads treat of the same subject, the doctrine of Brahman or Atman, and vary only in length and manner of treatment. There are about a dozen Upanishads of the three older Vedas and a great number of later treatises of the same name which are incorporated in the Atharvaveda. Distinguished by its age, length, and intrinsic importance is, before all, the Brihadaranyaka-Upanishad, and next to it Chandogya-Upanishad. More remarkable for their beauty than for their originality are Kathaka-Upanishad, Mandaka-Upanishad, and others.

FUNDAMENTAL IDEA OF THE UPANISHADS

11. Two terms, Brahman and Atman, form almost the only

objects of which the Upanishads speak. Very often they are treated as synonyms, but when a difference is noticeable, Brahman is the philosophical principle, as realised in the universe, and *Atman* the same, as realised in the soul. This presupposed, we might express the fundamental thought of all the Upanishads by the simple equation:

Brahman = Atman

that is, Brahman, the power from which all worlds proceed, in which they subsist, and into which they finally return, this eternal, omnipresent, omnipotent power is identical with our Atman, with that in each of us which we must consider as our true Self, the unchangeable essence of our being, our soul. This idea alone secures to the Upanishads an importance reaching far beyond their land and time; for whatever means of unveiling the secrets of Nature a future time may discover, this idea will be true for ever, from this mankind will never depart, if the mystery of Nature is to be solved, the key of it can be found only there where alone Nature allows us an interior view of the world, that is in ourselves.

CHRONOLOGY OF THE UPANISHADS

12. It can be proved that the Upanishads of the three first Vedas are older generally speaking than the Atharva Upanishads; of the former those in poetic form belong undoubtedly to a later period than those written in the old and simple prose style of the *Brahmanas;* among these again the two oldest are Brihadaranyaka and Chandogya, which contain the oldest Upanishad texts we posses. There are passages in *Chandogya* which may claim the priority over the parallel texts in *Brihadaranyaka,* but in most cases it can be clearly proved that passages in *Chandogya* are not only younger than the parallel texts in *Brihadaranyaka* but even dependent on them; this is evident from the fact that several passages of *Brihadaranyaka,* recur more or less literally in *Chandogya* but are no longer understood in their original meaning. In this way a careful comparison of the texts leads us to this results that in the whole Upanishad literature there are scarcely any texts older than those contained in *Brih-Up.* 1-4 which are connected with the person of Yajnavalkya; these either speak of him as is the case in 1, 4 and 2, 4, or reproduce his discourses with adversaries and his friend, the king Janaka, and take up the whole of the third and fourth book. In these passages we have the oldest germ of the doctrine of the Upanishads and consequently of Indian philosophy.

13. In the Yajnavalkya chapters of Brihadaranyaka and therefore in the oldest texts of Upanishads we find as the point of departure of the Upanishad doctrine a very bold idealism comparable to that of Parmenides in Greece, and culminating in the assertion that the *atman* is the only reality and that nothing exists beyond it. The whole doctrine may be summed up in three statements:—

1. The only reality is the *atman;*
2. The *atman* is the subject of knowledge in us;
3. The *atman* itself is unknowable.

1. All things in heaven and earth, gods, men, and other beings exist only in so far as they form a part of our *atman;* the *atman* must be seen, heard, known; he who sees, hears, and knows the *atman,* knows in it all that exists; as the sounds of a musical instrument cannot be grasped, but he who grasps the instrument, grasps also the sounds, so he who knows the *atman* knows in it all that exists; that man is lost and abandoned by gods and men, who believes in the existence of gods and men beyond the *atman.*
2. This *atman* is neither more nor less than the seer of seeing, the hearer of hearing, the knower of knowing, in a word the subject of knowledge in us, for this only is our real Self, which can never by any means be taken away from us.
3. The *atman,* as the subject of knowledge in us, is and remains unknowable in itself. "Thou canst not see the seer of seeing, thou canst not hear the hearer of hearing, thou canst not know the knower of knowing; how could a man know that by which he knows everything, how could he know the knower."

PANTHEISM

14. The idealism of Yajnavalkya denies, as we have seen, the existence of the world; but this denial could not be maintained in the long run. The reality of the world forced itself on the beholder, and the problem was to recognize it without abandoning the truth laid down by the sage Yajnavalkya. This led to a second stage of development which for want of a better name we may denominate Pantheism. Its chief doctrine is that the world is real, and yet the *atman* is the only reality, for the world is the *atman.* This is the most current thesis in the Upanishads and leads to very beautiful conceptions like that in *Chand.* 3, 14: "The

atman is my soul in the inner heart, smaller than a barley corn, smaller than a mustard-seed, smaller than a grain of millet; and he again is my soul in the inner heart, larger than the earth, larger than the atmosphere, larger than the heavens and all these worlds."

COSMOGONISM

13. The equation world = atman, notwithstanding its constant repetition in the Upanishads, is not a transparent one; for the *atman* is an absolute unity, and the world a plurality. How can they be regarded as identical? This difficulty may have led later on to the attempt to substitute for this incomprehensible identity another relation between *atman* and world, that of causality. This theory opened the way to a new interpretation of the old myths of creation which consider the principle, Prajapati or whatever it was, as the cause, and the world as the effect. Accordingly the cosmogonies of the Upanishads teach us that in the beginning the *atman* alone existed; the *atman* thought, "I will be manifold, I will send forth worlds", and created all these worlds. Having created them he entered into his creation as the soul, as the Upanishads never fail to emphasize. We have called this standpoint, finding no other name, Cosmogonism; some might propose to call it Theism, but from this it is essentially different. In the theistic view God creates the soul like everything else, but in the case before us the soul is not a creation of the *atman* but the *atman* himself, who enters into his creation as the individual soul.

THEISM

16. The identity of the highest and the individual *atman,* though perfectly true from the metaphysical standpoint, remains incomprehensible for the empirical view of things; this view distinguishes a plurality of souls different from each other and from the highest *atman,* the creative power of the universe. This distinction between the highest soul (paramatman) and the individual souls (jivatman) is the characteristic feature of what we may term the theism of certain later Upanishads. It emerges for the first time in *Kathaka* 3, 1, where the two, God and the soul, are contracted as light and shadow, which intimates that the latter has no reality of its own. But the constantly growing realistic tendencies went on sharpening this contrast, until in the Svetacvatara-Upanishad the highest soul, almighty and all-pervading as it is, is represented as essentially different from the individual soul which, limited and indigent, lives in the heart, smaller than the

point of a needle, smaller than the ten-thousandth part of a hair; and this, says the text, "becomes infinity". Even here God, though isolated and severed from the soul, lives together with it in the heart. As two birds living on the same tree, one of which feeds on the fruits of his works, while the other abstains from eating and only looks on; thus the individual soul, bewildered by his own impotence and grieving, looks for the help of the highest soul, or rather of his own divine and almighty self.

ATHEISM

17. Theism distinguishes three entities, a real world, a creative *atman* and the individual *atman* dependent on him. This duplication of the *atman* necessarily had a pernicious influence on one of the two branches, *viz*., on the highest *atman*, who in fact had always drawn his vital force from the soul living in us. Separated from this he became altogether superfluous, since the creative powers attributed to him could be transferred without difficulty to the primordial matter. Thus God disappeared and there remained only a primeval creative matter (prakriti) and opposed to it a plurality of individual souls (purusha), entangled in it by an inexplicable fate and striving to emancipate themselves from it by means of knowledge. This is exactly the standpoint of the Sankhya system. We see it shoot up more and more exuberantly in the later Upanishads, especially in Maitrayaniya; but its full development is only attained in the post-Vedic period and will be treated later. Before leaving the Veda we have to speak of the moral and eschatological consequences of the Vedic philosophy.

VEDIC ESCHATOLOGY BEFORE THE UPANISHADS

18. In contrast with the Semitic view, the belief in the immortality of the soul has been from the oldest times a patrimony of the Indo-Germanic race. Even in the oldest hymns of the Rigveda the hope is frequently expressed that after death good men will go to the gods to share their happy life. As for the wicked it is their destiny, only darkly hinted at, to fall into a deep abyss and disappear. The first mortal who found the way to the luminous heights of the happy other-world for all the following generations was Yama, who, as king of the blessed dead, sits with them under a leafy tree and passes the time in carousing; the analogous ideas of Jesus when He speaks of sitting at table with Abraham, Isaac, and Jacob in the future state are known to everybody. Different stages of happiness for pious worshippers seem not to have

been a part of the oldest creed. In the course of time this was modified and the belief arose that good and evil deeds find their corresponding rewards and punishments in a future life. A very striking passage of a *Brahmana* says: "Whatever food a man eats in this world, by that food he is eaten in the next world." Among the evils which await the bad man in the world to come we often find mentioned an indefinite fear of dying again and again even in the other world (punarmrityu). This notion of a repeated death led on to the idea that it must be preceded by a repeated life, and in transferring this repeated living and dying from the world beyond to the earth, the Hindu came finally to that dogma which has been in all subsequent ages more characteristic of India than anything else—the great doctrine of metempsychosis. The first passage where this creed clearly appears is in the *Brihadaranyaka-Up.*; and it discloses to us also the real motives of the remarkable dogma. Yajnavalkya, when asked what remains of man after death, takes the interrogator by the hand, leads him from the assembly to a solitary place, and reveals to him there the great secret: "and what they spoke was work, and what they praised was work; verily a man becomes holy by holy works, wicked by wicked works." This passage together with several others proves that the chief motive of the dogma of transmigration was to explain the different destinies of men by the supposition that they are the fruits of merit and demerit in a preceding life.

DEVELOPMENT OF THIS DOCTRINE IN THE UPANISHADS

19. A religion, after having come to a better view of things, cannot discard the preceding and less perfect steps of development which have led up to it. Thus the New Testament cannot emancipate itself from the Old Testament and its very different spirit. So too the Upanishads, after having come to the creed of metempsychosis, had to retain at the same time the old Vedic creed of rewards and punishments in the other world. The two views combined led to a complicated system, which taught a two-fold reward and punishment, the first in the world beyond, the second in a succeeding life on earth. This theory is fully explained in the so-called "doctrine of the Five Fires", an important text found both in *Chhandogya* 5 and in *Brihadaranyaka* 6. This combined theory of compensation distinguishes three ways after death—(1) the way of the fathers, (2) the way of the gods, and (3) the "third place".

(1) The way of the fathers, destined for the performer of pious works, leads through the smoke of the funeral pyre

and a series of "dark" stations to the placid realm of the moon, where the soul in commerce with the gods, enjoys the fruit of its good works, until they are consumed. As soon as the treasure of good works is exhausted, the soul, through the intermediate stations of ether, wind, fog, rain, plant, semen and womb passes to a new human existence, in which once more the good and evil works of the previous life find their reward.

(2) The way of the gods is destined for those who have spent their life in worshipping Brahman. They go through the flame of the funeral pyre and a series of "luminous" stations first to the sun, thence "to the moon, from the moon to the lightning; there is a spirit, he is not like a human being; he leads them to Brahman. For them there is no return." This passage evidently teaches that by the way of the gods is attained the highest goal, the union with Brahman. The later system, however, teaching that the knower of Brahman stands higher than the worshipper of Brahman, considers this union with Brahman, obtained by worshipping it, only as a step leading to the highest perfection, which the souls united with Brahman obtain only after receiving in it perfect knowledge.

(3) For those who have neither worshipped Brahman nor performed good works the "third place" is destined leading to a new life as lower animals—worms, insects, snakes etc., after a previous punishment in the different hells. This punishment in hell, which is a later addition, is not found in the Upanishads and appears first in the system of the Vedanta.

LIBERATION BY KNOWLEDGE

20. Transmigration is believed to be just as real as the empirical world. But from a higher point of view empirical reality together with creation and transmigration is only a great illusion; for in truth there is no manifold, no world, but only one being—the Brahman, the atman. The attainment of this knowledge is the highest aim of man and in its possession consists the final liberation. The knowledge is not the means of liberation, it is liberation itself. He who has attained the conviction "I am Brahman" has reached with it the knowledge that he in himself is the totality of all that is, and consequently he will not fear anything because there is nothing beyond him; he will not injure anybody, for nobody 'injures himself by himself.' There are, property speaking, no means of attaining this knowledge; it comes of itself; it is, in the view of the theistic Upanishads, a grace of God. He who has

obtained this knowledge continues to live, for he must consume the fruit of his preceding life; but life with its temptations can no longer delude him. By the fire of knowledge his former works are "burnt" and no new works can arise. He knows that his body is not his body, his works are not his works; for he is the totality of the *atman*, the divine being, and when he dies, "his spirit does not wander any more, for Brahman is he, and into Brahman he is resolved".

> "As rivers run and in the deep
> Lose name and form and disappear
> So goes, from name and form released,
> The wise man to the deity."

THIRD PERIOD

POST-VEDIC PHILOSOPHY

21. The thoughts of the Upanishads led in the post-Vedic period not only to the two great religions of Buddhism and Jainism but also to a whole series of philosophical systems. Six of these are considered as orthodox, because they are believed to be reconcileable with the Vedic creed, the others are rejected as heretical. The six orthodox systems are; (1) the Sankhyam of Kapila, (2) the Yoga of Patanjali, (3) the Nyaya of Gotama, (4) the Vaiceshikam of Kanada, (5) the Mimansa of Jaimini, (6) the Vedanta of Badarayana. As for the heterodox systems, the most important are Buddhism, Jainism, and the materialistic system of the Charvakas; several others are nothing more than the Vedantic views combined with the popular creeds of Vishnuism or Saivaism. But the six orthodox schools are not philosophical systems either in the strict sense of the term. The Mimansa is only a methodical handbook treating of the various questions arising out of the complicated Vedic ritual. The Yoga is a systematic exposition of the method of attaining union with the *atman* by means of concentration in oneself. The Nyaya, though it treats incidentally of all kinds of philosophical topics, is properly nothing more than a handbook of logic or better of disputation, furnishing a canon for use in controversies. The Vaiceshikam, giving a classification of existing things under six categories, is interesting enough, but more from a physical than a philosophical point of view. The only systems of metaphysical importance are the Sankhyam and the Vedanta; but even these are not to be considered as original creations of the philosophical mind, for the common basis of both and with them of Buddhism and Jainism is to be found in the Upanishads which by a kind of degeneration have developed

into Buddhism on one side and the Sankhya system on the other. Contrary to both, the later Vedanta of Badarayana and Sankara goes back to the Upanishads and founds on them that great system of the Vedanta which we have to consider as the ripest fruit of Indian wisdom.

THE PHILOSOPHY OF THE EPIC PERIOD

22. From the Veda to the later systems leads a philosophical development the history of which for want of special documents, must be supplied from the vast bulk of the Mahabharatam. Here we find, in the Bhagavadgita (Book vi.), the Sanatsujataparvan (Book v. 1565 ff.), the Mokshadharma (Book xii.) and other texts, the materials which, though in an earlier form than that of the *Mahabharatam,* have formed the common base of Buddhism and Sankhyam. The philosophical system of the *Mahabharatam,* whether we call it epic Sankhyam or realistic *Vedanta,* is the common mother of both. Some scholars maintain that the religion of Buddha is an offshoot of the Sankhyam. Both are right. Buddhism certainly precedes what we call now the Sankhya system, but it depends on what is called Sankhyam in the *Mahabharatam.* Originally Sankhyam (calculation, reflection) does not mean a certain philosophical system but philosophical enquiry in general; it is the opposite of Yoga, which means the attainment of the *atman* by means of concentration in oneself. The words are thus used where they occur for the first time (*Svet.* 6, 13), and it is an open question, demanding further research, whether not only in the *Bhagavadgita* but also throughout the *Mahabharatam* the words *Sankhyam* and *Yoga* are not so much names of philosophical systems as general terms for the two methods of reflection and concentration. Without entering into details we may say that even in the *Mahabharatam* the primordial matter (*prakriti*) is opposed to a plurality of souls (*purusha*); but both are more or less slightly dependent on Brahman as on the highest principle. This is the starting point both of the later Sankhyam which rejects Brahman as the connecting link, and of Buddhism which denies not only God but also the soul.

BUDDHISM

23. The success of Buddhism in India was due in part to the overwhelming personality of its founder, in part to the breaking down of caste prejudices by which he opened the road to salvation to the great masses of the population. Only in small measure did the Buddhism owe this success to the originality of its ideas, for almost all its essential theories had

their predecessors in the Vedic and epic periods. The fundamental idea of Buddhism, laid down in the four holy truths, is this—that we can extinguish the pains of existence only by extinguishing our thirst for existence. The same idea is put forth in the 12 Nidanas, which by a series of steps go back from the pains of life to the thirst for life and from this to ignorance as the ultimate cause of thirst and pain altogether. We see in these and many other Buddhistic ideas only a new form of what Yajnavalkya teaches in the *Brih.-Up.* and if Buddhism in its opposition to the Brahmanical creed goes so far as to deny soul, this denial is only apparent, since Buddhism maintains the theory of transmigration effected by *karman*, the work of the preceding existence. This *karman* must have in every case an individual bearer and that is what the Upanishads call the *atman* and what the Buddhists inconsistently deny. A common feature of Buddhism and Sankhyam is that they both regard pain as the starting point of philosophical enquiry, thus clearly showing the secondary character of both. For philosophy has its root in the thirst for knowledge and it is a symptom of decadence in India as in Greece when it begins to be considered as a remedy for the pains of life.

THE LATER SANKHYA SYSTEM

24. There are many other features in the Sankhya system which show clearly that it is not, as has been generally held up to the present, the original creation of an individual philosophical genius, but only the final result of a long process of degeneration, as has already been shown. The theism of the Upanishads had separated the highest soul from the individual soul, opposing to them a primordial matter. After the elimination of the highest soul there remained two principles—(1) prakriti, primeval matter, and (2) a plurality of purushas or subjects of knowledge. This dualism, as the starting-point of the Sankhya system, is in itself quite incomprehensible; it becomes intelligible only by its development as shown before. The aim of man is the emancipation of the *purusha* from the *prakriti;* and this is attained by the knowledge that *purusha* and *prakriti* are totally different, and that all the pains of life, being only modifications of *prakriti*, do not affect the *purusha* in the least. To awaken this consciousness in the purusha, prakriti unfolds its essence to it anew in every life, producing by gradual evolution the cosmic intellect (Mahan or Buddhi), from this the principle of individuation (Ahankara), from this mind, organs of sense, and the rudiments, and from the latter

material objects. The *purusha* beholds this evolution of *prakriti;* if he understands that *prakriti* is different from himself he is emancipated, if not he remains in the circle of transmigration and suffering. The whole system seems to be based on an original assumption that there is only one *purusha* and one *prakriti* by the separation of which the final aim is attained for both. The pretended plurality of *purushas* looks like a later addition; and we do not understand how the one and indivisible *prakriti* develops its being before every single *purusha* again and again to help him in his emancipation, if there always remains an innumerable quantity of unemancipated *purushas*. If we add to this the fact that all the other elements of the system including the three gunas can be derived from the Upanishad doctrine, we can no longer hesitate to admit that the whole Sankhya system is nothing but a result of the degeneration of the Vedanta by means of the growth of realistic tendencies. There seems to have been a time when Vedantic thought lived only in this realistic form of the Sankhya; for when the Yoga took the form of a philosophical system it was built up on the very inconvenient base of the Sankhya system, probably because at that time no other base was available.

THE SYSTEM OF THE VEDANTA

2. The genesis of the Vedanta-system, represented by Badarayana and Sankara, has many analogies with the Reformation in the Christian Church. In the same way as Luther and others rejected the various traditions of the medieval Church and based the Protestant creed on the pure word of the Bible, so Sankara (born 788 A.D.) rejected the changes in Vedic doctrine brought about by Buddhism and Sankhya and founded the great system that bears his name on the holy word of the Upanishads alone; but in doing this a great difficulty arose; for the Upanishads, the words of which are in the view of Sankara a divine revelation, contain not only the pure idealism of Yajnavalkya but also its later modifications such as pantheism, cosmogonism and theism. In meeting the difficulty Sankara exhibits great philosophical astuteness, which may serve as a model for Christian theology in future times; he distinguishes throughout an esoteric system (paravidya) containing a sublime philosophy, and an exoteric system (aparavidya) embracing, under the wide mantle of a theological creed all the fanciful imaginings which spring in course of time from the original idealism. The exoteric system gives a description of the Brahman in the richest colours, treat-

ing it in part as the pantheistic soul of the world, and in part as a personal god; it gives a full account of the periodical creation and reabsorption of the world and of the never-ending circle of transmigration, etc. The esoteric system on the contrary maintains with Yajnavalkya that Brahman, or the *atman* is absolutely unknowable and attainable only by the concentration of *yoga,* that there is from the highest standpoint neither creation nor world, neither transmigration nor plurality of souls, and that complete liberation is reached by him and by him alone who has awakened to the beatific consciousness, expressed in the words of the Upanishads: "Aham Brahma asmi" (I am Brahman).

Thus the Indians in their Vedanta possess a theological and philosophical system satisfying not only the wants of the people, but also the demands of a mind accessible to true knowledge only in its purest form.

THE PHILOSOPHY OF THE VEDANTA

On my journey through India I have noticed with satisfaction, that in philosophy till now our brothers in the East have maintained a very good tradition, better perhaps, than the more active but less contemplative branches of the great Indo-Aryan family in Europe, where Empirism, Realism and their natural consequence, Materialism, grow from day to day more exuberantly, whilst metaphysics, the very centre and heart of serious philosophy, are supported only by the few who have learned to brave the spirit of the age.

In India the influence of this perverted and perversive spirit of our age has not yet overthrown in religion and philosophy the good traditions of the great ancient time. It is true, that most of the ancient *darcana's* even in India find only an historical interest; followers of the Sankhya-System occur rarely; Nyaya is cultivated mostly as an intellectual sport and exercise, like grammer or mathematics,—but the Vedanta is, now as in the ancient time, living in the mind and heart of every thoughtful Hindu. It is true, that even here in the sanctuary of Vedantic metaphysics, the realistic tendencies, natural to man, have penetrated, producing the misinterpreting variations of Sankara's Advaita, known under the names Vicishtadvaita, Dvaita, Suddhadvaita of Ramanuja, Madhva, Vallabha,—but India till now has not yet been seduced by their voices, and of hundred Vedantins (I have it from a well informed man, who is himself a zealous adversary of Sankara and follower of Ramanuja) fifteen perhaps adhere to Ramanuja, five to Madhva, five to Vallabha, and seventy-five to Sankaracharya.

This fact may be for poor India in so many misfortunes a great consolation; for the eternal interests are higher than the temporary ones; and the System of the Vedanta, as founded on the Upanishads and Vedanta Sutras and accomplished by Sankara's commentaries on them,—equal in rank to Plato and Kant—is one of the most valuable products of the genius of mankind in his researches of the eternal truth,—as I propose to show now by a short sketch of Sankara's Advaita and by comparing its principal doctrines with the best that occidental philosophy has produced till now.

Taking the Upanishads, as Sankara does, for revealed truth with absolute authority, it was not an easy task to build out of their materials a consistent philosophical system, for the Upanishads are in Theology, Cosmology and Psychology full of the hardest contradictions. So in many passages the nature of Brahman is painted in various and luxuriant colours, and again we read, that the nature of Brahman is quite unattainable to human words, to human understanding;—so we meet sometimes long reports explaining how the world has been created by Brahman, and again we are told, that there is no world besides Brahman, and all variety of things is mere error and illusion;—so we have fanciful descriptions of the Samsara, the way of the wandering soul up to the heaven and back to the earth, and again we read, that there is no Samsara, no variety of souls at all, but only one Atman, who is fully and totally residing in every being.

Sankara in these difficulties created by the nature of his materials, in face of so many contradictory doctrines, which he was not allowed to decline and yet could not admit altogether,—has found a wonderful device, which deserves the attention, perhaps the imitation of the Christian dogmatists in their embarassments. He constructs out of the materials of the Upanishads two systems, one esoteric, philosophical (called by him *nirguna vidya,* sometimes *paramarthika avastha*) containing the metaphysical truth for the few ones, rare in all times and countries, who are able to understand it; and another exoteric, theological (*saguna vidya, vyavahariki avastha*) for the general public, who want images, not abstract truth, worship, not meditation.

I shall now point out briefly the two systems, esoteric and exoteric, in pursuing and confronting them through the four chief parts, which Sankara's system contains, and every complete philosophical system must contain:

I. Theology, the doctrine of God or of the philosophical principle.
II. Cosmology, the doctrine of the world.
III. Psychology, the doctrine of the soul.
IV. Eschatology, the doctrine of the last things, the things after death.

THEOLOGY

The Upanishads swarm with fanciful and contradictory descriptions of the nature of Brahman. He is the all-pervading akasa, is the purusha in the sun, the purusha in the eye; his head is the heaven, his eyes are sun and moon, his breath is the wind, his footstool the earth; he is infinitely great as soul of the universe and infinitely small as the soul in us; he is in particular the *icvara,* the personal God, distributing justly reward and punishment according to the deeds of man. All these numerous descriptions are collected by Sankara under the wide mantle of the exoteric theology, the *saguna vidya* of Brahman, consisting of numerous "vidyas" adapted for approaching the eternal being not by the way of knowledge but by the way of worshipping, and having each its particular fruits. Mark, that also the conception of God as a personal being, an *icara,* is merely exoteric and does not give us an adequate knowledge of the Atman;—and indeed, when we consider what is personality, how narrow in its limitations, how closely connected which egotism, the counter part of godly essence, who might think so low of God, to impute him personality?

In the sharpest contrast to these exoteric vidyas stands the esoteric *nirguna vidya* of the Atman; and its fundamental tenet is the absolute inaccessibility of God to human thoughts and words;

yato vaco nivartante
aprapya manasa saha

and again:

avijnatam vijanatam
vijnatam avijanatam

and the celebrated formula occurring so often in Brihadaranyaka-Upanishad: *neti! neti!* viz., whatever attempts you make to know the Atman, whatever description you give of him, I always say: *na iti, na iti,* it is not so, it is not so! therefore the wise Bahva, when asked by the king Vashkalin, to explain the Brahman, kept silence. And when the king repeated his request again and again, the rishi broke out into the answer: "I tell it you, but you don't understand it; *canto 'yam atma,* this Atma is silence!" We know it now by the Kantian philosophy, that the answer of Bahva was correct, we know it, that the very organisation of our intellect (which is bound once for ever to its innate forms of perception, space, time, and causality) excludes us from a knowledge of the spaceless, timeless, godly reality for ever and ever. And yet the Atman, the only godly being is not unattainable to us, is even not far from us, for we have it fully and totally in ourselves as our own metaphysical entity; and here, when returning from the outside and apparent world to the deepest secrets of our own nature, we may come to God, not by knowledge, but by *anubhava,* by absorption into our own self. There is a great difference between knowledge, in which subject and object are distinct from each other, and anubhava, where subject and object coincide in the same. He who by anubhava comes to the great intelligence, *"aham brahma asmi"*, obtains a state called by Sankara *Samradhanam,* accomplished satisfaction; and indeed, what might he desire, who feels and knows himself as the sum and totality of all existence!

COSMOLOGY

Here again we meet the distinction of exoteric and esoteric doctrine, though not so clearly severed by Sankara as in other parts of his system.

The exoteric Cosmology according to the natural but erroneous realism (*avidya*) in which we are born, considers this world as the reality, and can express its entire dependency on Brahman only by the mythical way of a creation of the world by Brahman. So a temporal creation of the world, even as in the Christian documents, is also taught in various and well-known passages of the Upanishads. But such a creation of the material world by an immaterial cause, performed in a certain point of time after an eternity elapsed uselessly, is not only against the demands of human reason and natural science, but also against another important doctrine of the Vedanta, which teaches and must teach (as we shall see hereafter) the "beginninglessness of the migration of souls", *samsarasya anaditvam.* Here the expedient of Sankara is very clever and worthy of imitation. Instead of the temporary creation once for ever of the Upanishads, he teaches that the world in great periods is created and reabsorbed by Brahman (referring to the misunderstood verse of the Rigveda[1]); this mutual crea-

1 *Surya Candramasau dhata yathapurvan akalpayat.*

tion and reabsorption lasts from eternity, and no creation can be allowed by our system to be the first and that for good reasons, as we shall see just now.—If we ask: *Why* has God created the world? the answers to this question are generally very unsatisfactory. For his own glorification? How may we attribute to him so much vanity!—For his particular amusement? But he was an eternity without this plaything!—For love of mankind? How may he love a thing before it exists, and how may it be called love, to create millions for misery and eternal pain!—The Vedanta has a better answer. The never ceasing new-creation of the world is a moral necessity cannected with the central and most valuable doctrine of the exoteric Vedanta, the doctrine of Samsara.

Man, says Sankara, is like a plant. He grows, flourishes and at the end he dies; but not totally. For as the plant, when dying, leaves behind it the seed, from which, according to its quality, a new plant grows,—so man, when dying, leaves his *karma,* the good and bad works of his life, which must be rewarded and punished in another life after this. No life can be the first, for it is the fruit of previous actions, nor the last, for its actions must be expiated in a next following life. So the Samsara is without beginning and without end, and the new creation of the world after every absorption into Brahman is a moral necessity. I need not point out, in India less than anywhere, the high value of this doctrine of Samsara as a consolation in the afflictions as a moral agent in the temptations of life,—I have to say here only, that the Samsara, though not the absolute truth, is a mythical representative of a truth which in itself is unattainable to our intellect; mythical is this theory of metempsychosis only in so far as it invests in the forms of space and time what really is spaceless and timeless, and therefore beyond the reach of our understanding. So the Samsara is just so far from the truth, as the *saguna vidya* is from the *nirguna vidya;* it is the eternal truth itself, but (since we cannot conceive it otherwise) the truth in an allegorical form, adapted to our human understanding. And this is the character of the whole exoteric Vedanta, whilst the esoteric doctrine tries to find out the philosophical, the absolute truth.

And so we come to the esoteric Cosmology, whose simple doctrine is this, that in reality there is no manifold world, but only Brahman, and that what we consider as the world, is a mere illusion (*maya*) similar to a *mrigatrishnika,* which disappears when we approach it and not more to be feared than the rope, which we took in the darkness for a serpent. There are, as you see, many similes in the Vedanta, to illustrate the illusive character of this world, but the best of them is perhaps, when Sankara compares our life with a long dream;—a man whilst dreaming does not doubt oft the reality of the dream, but this reality disappears in the moment of awakening, to give place to a truer reality, which we were not aware of whilst dreaming. The life a dream! this has been the thought of many wise men from Pindar and Sophocles to Shakespere and Calderon de la Barca, but nobody has better explained this idea, than Sankara. And indeed, the moment when we die may be to nothing so similar as to the awakening from a long and heavy dream; it may be, that then heaven and earth are blown away like the nightly phantoms of the dream, and what then may stand before us? or rather in us? Brahman, the eternal reality, which was hidden to us till then by this dream of life!—This world is maya, is illusion; is not the very reality, that is the deepest thought of the esoteric Vedanta, attained not by calculating *tarka* but by *anubhava*, by returning from this variegated world to the deep recess of our own self (*Atman*). Do so, if you can, and you will get aware of a reality very different from empirical reality, a timeless, spaceless, changeless reality, and you will feel and experience that whatever is outside of this only true reality, is mere appearance, is maya, is a dream!—This was the way the Indian thinkers went, and by a similar way, shown by Parmenides, Plato came to the same truth, when knowing and teaching that this world is a world of shadows, and that the reality is not in these shadows, but behind them. The accord here of Platonism and Vedantism is wonderful, but both have grasped this great metaphysical truth by intuition; their tenet is true, but they are not able to prove it, and in so far they are defective. And here a great light and assistance to the Indian and the Greek thinker comes from the philosophy of Kant, who went quite another way, not the Vedantic and Platonic way of intuition, but the way of abstract reasoning and scientific proof. The great work of Kant is an analysis of human mind, not in the superficial way of Locke, but going to the very bottom of it. And in doing so, Kant found, to the surprise of the world and of himself, that three essential elements of this outside world, viz., space, time, and causality, are not, as we naturally believe, eternal fundamentals of an objective reality, but merely subjective innate perceptual forms of our own intellect. This has been proved by Kant and by his great disciple Schopenhauer with mathematical evidence, and I have given these proofs (the base of all scientific metaphysics) in the shortest and clearest form in my *Elemente der Metaphysik*—a book which I am resolved now to get translated into English,[1] for the benefit not of the Europeans (who may learn German) but of my brothers in India, who will be greatly astonished to find in Germany the scientific substruction of their own philosophy, the Advaita Vedanta! For Kant has demonstrated, that space, time and causality are not objective realities, but only subjective forms of our intellect, and the unavoidable conclusion is this, that the world, as far as it is extended in space, running on in time, ruled throughout by causality, in so far is merely a representation of my mind and nothing beyond it. You see the concordance of Indian, Greek and German metaphysics; the world is maya, is illusion, says *Sankara;*—it is a world of shadows, not of realities; says *Plato;*—it is "appearance only, not the thing in itself", says *Kant*. Here we have the same doctrine in three different parts of the world, but the scientific proofs of it are not in Sankara, not in Plato, but only in Kant.

PSYCHOLOGY

Here we convert the order and begin with the esoteric Psychology, because it is closely connected with the esoteric Cosmology and its fundamental doctrine: the world is *maya*. All is illusive, with one exception, with the exception of my own Self, of my Atman. My Atman cannot be illusive, as Sankara shows, anticipating the *"cogito, ergo sum"* of Descartes,—for he who would deny it, even in denying it, witnesses its reality. But what is the relation bettween my individual soul, the Jiva-Atman, and the highest soul, the Parama-Atman or Brahman? Here Sankara, like a prophet, foresees the deviations of Ramanuja, Madava and Vallabha and refutes them in showing, that the Jiva cannot be a part of Brahman (Ramanuja), because Brahman is without parts (for it is timeless and spaceless, and all parts are either successions in time or coordinations in space,—as we may add),—neither a different thing from Brahman (Madhva), for Brahman is *ekam eva advitiyam*, as we may experience by *anubhava*,—nor a metamorphose of Brahman (Vallabha), for Brahman is unchangeable (for, as we know now by Kant, it is out of causality). The conclusion is, that the Jiva being neither a part nor a different thing, nor a variation of Brahman, must be the Paramatman fully and totally himself, a conclusion made equally by the Vedantin Sankara, by the Platonic Plotinos,

1 The Elements of Metaphysics, translated into English by C. M. Duff, London, 1894.

and by the Kantian Schopenhauer. But Sankara in his conclusions goes perhaps further than any of them. If really our soul, says he, is not a part of Brahman but Brahman himself, then all the attributes of Brahman, all-pervadingness, eternity, all-mightiness (scientifically spoken: exemption of space, time, causality) are ours; *aham brahma asmi*, I am Brahman, and consequently I am all-pervading (spaceless), eternal (timeless), almighty (not limited in my doing by causality). But these godly qualities are hidden in me, says Sankara, as the fire is hidden in the wood, and will appear only after the final deliverance.

What is the cause of this concealment of my godly nature? The Upadhi's, answers Sankara, and with this answer we pass from the esoteric to the exoteric psychology. The Upadhi's are manas and indriya's, prana with its five branches, sukshmam cariram,—in short, the whole psychological apparatus, which together with a factor changeable from birth to birth, with my karman, accompanies my Atman in all his ways of migration, without infecting his godly nature, as the crystal is not infected by the colour painted over it. But wherefrom originate these Upadhi's? They form of course part of the *maya*, the great world-illusion, and like *maya* they are based on our innate *avidya* or ignorance, a merely negative power and yet strong enough to keep us from our godly existence. But now, from where comes this *avidya*, this primeval cause of ignorance, sin, and misery? Here all philosophers in India and Greece and everywhere have been defective, until Kant came to show us that the whole question is inadmissible. You ask for the cause of *avidya*, but it has no cause; for causality goes only so far as this world of the Samsara goes, connecting each link of it with another, but never beyond Samsara and its fundamental characteristic, the *avidya*. In enquiring after a cause of *avidya* with *maya*, Samsara and Upadhi's, you abuse, as Kant may teach us, your innate mental organ of causality to penetrate into a region for which it is not made, and where it is no more available. The fact is, that we are here in ignorance, sin and misery, and that we know the way out of them, but the question of a cause for them is senseless.

ESCHATOLOGY

And now a few words about this way out of the Samsara, and first about the exoteric theory of it. In the ancient time of the hymns there was no idea of Samsara but only rewards in heaven and (somewhat later punishments in a dark region (*padam gabhiram*), the precursor of the later hells. Then the deep theory of Samsara came up, teaching rewards and punishment in the form of a new birth on earth. The Vedanta combines both theories, and so it has a double expiation, first in heaven and hell, and then again in a new existence on the earth. This double expiation is different (1) for performers of good works, going the *pitriyana,* (2) for worshippers of the sagunam brahma, going the *devayana,* (3) for wicked deeds, leading to what is obscurely hinted at in the Upanishads as the *tritiyam sthanam,* the third place. (1) The *pitriyana* leads through a succession of dark spheres to the moon, there to enjoy the fruit of the good works and, after their consumption, back to an earthly existence. (2) The *devayana* leads through a set of brighter sphere to Brahman, without returning to the earth.[1] But this Brahman is only sagunam brahma, the object of worshipping, and its true worshippers, though entering into this sagunam brahma without returning, have to wait in it until they get *moksha* by obtaining *samyagdarcanam,* the full knowledge of the nirgunam brahma. (3) The *tritiyam sthanam,* including the later theories of hells, teaches punishment in them, and again punishment by returning to earth in the form of lower castes, animals, and plants. All these various and fantastical ways of Samsara are considered as true, quite as true as this world is, but not more. For the whole world and the whole way of Samsara is valid and true for those only who are in the *avidya,* not for those who have overcome it, as we have to show now.

The esoteric Vedanta does not admit the reality of the world nor of the Samsara, for the only reality is Brahman, seized in ourselves as our own Atman. The knowledge of this Atman, the great intelligence: *"aham brahma asmi"*, does not produce *moksha* (deliverance), but is *moksha itself.* Then we obtain what the Upanishad say

bhidyate hrdayagranthis
chidyante sarvasamsayah
kshiyante casya karmani
tasmin drste paravare.

When seeing Brahma as the highest and the lowest everywhere, all knots of our heart, all sorrows are split, all doubts vanish, and our works become nothing. Certainly no man can live without doing work, and so also the *Jivanmukta;* but he knows, that all these works are illusive, as this whole world is, and therefore they do not adhere to him nor produce for him a new life after death.—And what kind of work may such a man do?—People have often reproached the Vedanta with

1 *Jesam na punaravrthih.*

being defective in morals, and indeed. the Indian genius is too contemplative to speak much of deeds; but the fact is nevertheless, that the highest and purest morality is the immediate consequence of the Vedanta. The Gospels fix quite correctly as the highest law of morality: "love your neighbour as yourselves." But why should I do so, since by the order of nature I feel pain and pleasure only in myself, not in my neighbour? The answer is not in the Bible (this venerable book being not yet quite free of Semitic realism), but it is in the Veda, is in the great formula *"tat tvam asi"*, which gives in three words metaphysics and morals altogether. You shall love your neighbour as yourselves,—because you are your neighbour, and mere illusion makes you believe, that your neighbour is something different from yourselves. Or in the words of the Bhagavadgita: he, who knows himself in everything and everything in himself, will not injure himself by himself, *na hinasti atmana atmanam*. This is the sun and tenor of all morality; and this is the standpoint of a man knowing himself as Brahman. He feels himself everything,—so he will not desire anything, for he has whatever can be had;—he feels himself everything,—so he will not injure anything, for nobody injures himself. He lives in the world, is surrounded by its illusions but not deceived by them: like the man suffering from *timira*, who sees two moons but knows that there is one only, so the Jivanmukta sees the manifold world and cannot get rid of seeing it, but he knows, that there is only one being, Brahman, the Atman, his own Self; and he verifies it by his deeds of pure disinterested morality. And so he expects his end, as the potter expects the end of the twirling of his wheel, after the vessel is ready. And then, for him, when death comes, no more Samsara.[1] He enters into brahman, like the streams into the ocean:

> *yatha nadyah syandamanah samudre*
> *astam gacchanti namarupe vihaya*
> *tatha vidvan namarupad vimuktah*
> *paratparam purusam upaiti divyam.*

he leaves behind him *nama* and *rupam*, he leaves behind him *individuality*, but he does not leave behind him is *Atman*. his Self. It is not the falling of the drop into the infinite ocean, it is the whole ocean, becoming free from the fetters of ice, returning from its frozen state to that what it is really and has never ceased to be, to its own all-pervading, eternal, all-mighty nature.

And so the Vedanta, in its pure and unfalsified form, is the strongest support of pure morality, is the greatest consolation in the sufferings of life and death,—Indians, keep to it!—

1 *Na tasya prana utkramanti Brahma eva san Brahmapyeti.*

VEDANTASARA

INTRODUCTORY STANZA

To the Self, existent, intelligence, bliss, impartite, beyond the range of speech and thought, the substrate of all, I resort for the attainment of the desired thing.[1]

NOTES ON INTRODUCTORY STANZA

"All philosophy strives after unity. It is its aim, its task, to reduce complexity to simplicity, the many to the one."[2] The Upanishads tell us that this was the aim of Indian philosophers, and they not always Brahmans, in very early times. In the *Mundaka,* for example, it is related that the illustrious son of Sunaka approached the sage Angiras with due ceremony, and inquired of him what that was which, being known, all things would be known. He was told in reply that the wise regard "the invisible, intangible, unrelated, colourless one, who has neither eyes nor ears, neither hands nor feet, eternal, all-pervading, subtile and undecaying, as the source of all things." This is, of course, Brahma,[3] the so-called Absolute of the Vedanta, the Self of the verse before us; and the system then evolved from the inner consciousness of those early thinkers, but modified it would seem by Sankaracharya, and so stereotyped by his successors, continues to the present day; and not only so, but whilst the other five schools have well-nigh ceased to exert any appreciable influence, this "has overspread the whole land, overgrown the whole Hindu mind and life."[4]

In this opening verse Brahma is described as

1. *Existent (sat).*

The Vedanta postulates three kinds of existence, which it terms true (*paramarthika*), practical (*vyavaharika*), and apparent (*pratibhasika*). Brahma is the sole representative of the first. The second includes Iswara, individual souls, heaven, hell, and all phenomena. These are said to be imagined by ignorance, and to have no more true existence than things seen in a dream; but men have practical dealings with them as if they truly existed, so they are admitted to exist practically or conventionally. The third class comprises such things as a mirage, nacre mistaken for silver, or a snake imagined in a rope, which are the result of some defect, such

1 Emancipation.

2 *Anti-Theistic Theories*, p. 410.

3 This word is neuter, and must not be confounded with the masculine Brahma, a member of the Hindu triad. It is derived from the root *Brih,* 'to grow or increase,' and "perhaps its earliest signification was *the expansive force of nature,* regarded as a spiritual power, the power manifested most fully in vegetable, animal, and human life, but everywhere present, though unseen."—*Calcutta Review,* vol. lxvi, p. 14.

4 *Anti-Theistic Theories,* p. 341.

as short-sight, &c., in addition to ignorance. Yet it is believed that "when a man on seeing nacre, takes it for silver, apparent silver is *really produced!*" All these then are, from certain standpoints, real existences; but, to him who has true knowledge, the first alone is real.[1] This theory of existences is intended to explain away the finite and establish the infinite; but it cannot be admitted to have been successful. The existence of an invisible Being, who is entirely out of relation to the world, and devoid of apprehension, will, activity, and all other qualities, cannot possibly be established.

2. *Intelligence* (*chit* or *chaitanya*).

This is the most common synonym of Brahma, but he is also spoken of—as, for example, in the *Taittiriya Upanishad* (p. 56)—as 'cognition' or 'knowledge' (*jnana*). It must, however, be clearly understood that *he is not a cognizer or intelligent.* In commenting on the passage of the Upanishad just referred to, Sankaracharya says:—"Knowledge is here an abstract, indicating cognition, not the cognitive subject, being predicated of the ultimate along with truth and infinity. Truth and infinity would be incompatible with it did it imply a subject of cognition. If the pure idea were susceptible of modifications, how could it be pure and infinite? That is infinite which cannot be demarcated in any direction. If it were a knowing subject, it would be limited by its objects and its cognitions. . . . The knowledge of the absolute spirit, like the light of the sun, or like the heat in fire, is nought else than the absolute essence itself."[2]

In the *Mandukya Upanishad* (ver. 7), too, Brahma is said to be "neither[3] internally nor externally cognitive, neither conscious nor unconscious." This tenet is a necessity. For if Brahma were conscious, there would be objects of consciousness, which would involve dualism; for "wherever there is consciousness there is relation, and wherever there is relation there is dualism."[4] The Hindu pantheist, therefore, allying himself with "a scepticism which denies the validity of the primary perceptions and fundamental laws of mind,"[5] calmly annihilates the phenomenal; and with it his own self-consciousness, by calling it all illusory. It must be understood that the only ground for supposing Brahma to be 'intelligence,' is, that, in the state of practical existence, cognition of an object can only be effected by means of the internal organ, and that organ is declared to be itself unintelligent and to need an illuminator. The self-luminous Brahma is that illuminator! "It is not meant, however, that Brahma, by a voluntary exercise of his power, illumines that organ, for Brahma has no such power. The idea intended is, that the internal organ, simply by reason of its proximity to Brahma, who is unconscious, becomes illuminated, just as iron moves when brought near the magnet."[6] 'Intelligence,' therefore, means simply 'self-

1 *Rational Refutation*, sec. iii. chap. 1.
2 *Calcutta Review*. vol. lxvi. p. 19.
3 *Ibid.*, p. 29.
4 *Anti-Theistic Theories*, p. 423.
5 *Ibid.*, p. 419.
6 *Rational Refutation*, pp. 214-216.

luminousness,' and its existence is surmised merely on the ground named above! But the internal organ[1] is a portion of the phenomenal, and therefore illusory. So too must be its illuminator. Brahma, therefore, as 'intelligence,' is not established.

3. *Bliss* (*ananda*).

This has been characterised as "a bliss without the fruition of happiness," and rightly so. For absorption into Brahma is described as a permanent state "resembling precisely that of deep sleep,"—"a condition of insensibility,"—in which the emancipated spirit is without a body, mind, or cognition! Where is there any room in such a state for joy? "But what, in that case," says the author of the *Sankhya-pravachana-bhashya,* "becomes of the scripture which lays down that soul is happiness? The answer is: 'Because of there being *cessation of misery,* only in a loose acceptation does the term happiness denote soul.' ... To move ambition in the dull or ignorant, the emancipated state, which really is *stoppage of misery,* Soul itself, is lauded to them by the Veda as happiness."[2] Brahma, then, as joy, is wholly a product of the imagination.

4. *Impartite* (*akhanda*).

According to the commentator *Nrisimhasarasvati,* this term means "devoid of anything of a like kind or of a different kind, and without internal variety. A tree, for example, has the 'internal variety' of leaves, flowers, and fruit; it has things 'of a like kind,' in other trees —and things 'of a different kind,' in stones,[3] &c. But Brahma is not so, he being absolute and unchangeable unity. It is from the standpoint of true existence that he is regarded as impartite and solitary; for, from that of practical existence, he is appropriated to countless internal organs and underlies all phenomena.

5. *Substrate of all* (*akhiladhara*).

He is the substrate only in the way that nacre is of apparent silver, or that a rope is of the snake imagined in it; and, like the silver and the snake, the world is but a *vivartta* or illusory effect. Its illusory-material cause is Brahma, and ignorance its material cause. The writers of the Upanishads, *i.e.,* the Vedantists of the old school, were undoubtedly *parinamavadins,* or believers in the *reality* of the world of perception; and, with them, Brahma was not its substrate or illusory-material cause, but the material from which it was evolved or developed, as the web from a spider, as foam from water, or as curd from milk.[4] The passage quoted above from the Mundaka Upanishad seems clearly to teach this doctrine when setting forth Brahma as the absolute unity, which being known, all things are known; and the context adds that "as a spider throws out and retracts [its web], as herbs spring up in the ground, and as hair is produced on the living person, so is the universe derived from the undecaying

1 In Sanskrit, *antahkarana.* It consists of *manas, buddhi, ahankara* and *chitta,* and yet is unintelligent!
2 *Rational Refutation,* pp. 33, 34.
3 *Panchadasi,* ii. 20.
4 *Miscellaneous Essays,* i. 375, 376.

one" (i. 1, 7). It seems to be distinctly taught, too, in the *Chhandogya Upanishad.* The sixth book opens with a dialogue between a Brahman named Aruni and his son Svetaketu, who, at twenty-four years of age, has returned home on the completion of a twelve years' course of Vedic study. Seeing him full of conceit, his father asks him whether he had sought from his teacher that instruction by which the unheard becomes heard, the unthought thought, the unknown known. On the son's confessing that he had not sought it, the father says, "My dear, as by one clod of clay all that is made of clay is known, the difference being only a name, arising from speech, but the truth being that all is clay; and as, my dear, by one nugget of gold all that is made of gold is known, the difference being only a name, arising from speech, but the truth being that all is gold; and as, my dear, by one pair of nail-scissors all that is made of iron is known, the difference being only a name, arising from speech, but the truth being that all is iron—thus, my dear, is that instruction."[1] That is to say, Brahma being known as material cause, all things are known. The son then remarks that his teacher could not have known this doctrine, and asks his father to explain it further. The latter then goes on to say, "In the beginning, my dear, this was the existent, one only, without a second. Some say that in the beginning, this was the non-existent, one only, without a second; and from the non-existent the existent arose. But how could it be thus, my dear; how could the existent arise from the non-existent? In the beginning, my dear, this was indeed the existent, one only, without a second." Sankaracharya says that 'this'[2] refers to 'the universe' (*jagat*), and that 'in the beginning' means 'before production' (*pragutpatteh*). The drift of the passage then surely is that this world, *a reality,* before its evolution, existed potentially in Brahma, its material cause. It, in fact, "proves the reality of the cause from the reality of the effect, and so declares the reality, not the falseness of all."[3] In the same Upanishad (iii. 14, 1), we find the words, "All this is indeed Brahma, being produced from, resolved into, and existing in him;" and the opening words of the *Aitareya Upanishad* are, "In the beginning this was the self, one only;" and in both cases, as before, 'this' is said to refer to the world of perception, which is treated as a reality.

In his valuable essay on the Vedanta, Colebrooke shows, by ample quotations, that, this view of the world's reality and of Brahma's material causativity was propounded by the early Vedantic teachers, including Sankaracharya himself; and he considered the doctrine of Maya, or the world's unreality, to be "a graft of a later growth," uncountenanced by the aphorisms of the Vedanta or by the gloss of Sankaracharya. The learned editor of the new edition of Colebrooke's essays thinks this "hardly correct" as regards Sankara,

1 *Sacred Books of the East,* i. 92.

2 Prof. Max Muller, in his translation, omits 'this' altogether, and so completely changes the sense of the passage.

3 *Aphorisms of Sandilya,* translated by Cowell, p. 42.

but adds, "There can hardly be a question as to the fact that the original *Vedanta* of the earlier *Upanishads* and of the *Sutras* did not recognize the doctrine of *Maya*. The earliest school seems to have held Brahma to be the material cause of the world in a grosser sense." As regards Sankaracharya, the fact is that different portions of his comments on the aphorisms are mutually conflicting. For example, in one place he ridicules the idea of an infinite series of works and worlds subsisting in the relation of cause and effect, and then, elsewhere, distinctly advocates it. Again, when opposing the idealism of the Buddhists, he strongly maintains the *reality* of objects of perception, rebutting the objections advanced against it, and supports the tenet of the material causativity of Brahma; whilst on another occasion he accepts the theory of *Maya*.[1]

6. *'Beyond the range of speech or thought.'*

The following are some of the Vedic texts on this point:—"From whom words turn back, together with the mind, not reaching him" (*Taittiriya,* ii. 9). "The eye goes not thither, nor speech, nor mind" (*Kena,* i. 3). "Nnthinkable, unspeakable" (*Mandukya,* 7).

The Vedantist creed, as held since the time of Sankaracharya, *i.e.,* during the last thousand years, may, then, be thus summed up:—"Brahma alone—a spirit; essentially existent, intelligence and joy; void of all qualities and of all acts; in whom there is no consciousness such as is denoted by 'I,' 'thou,' and 'it;' who apprehends no person or thing, nor is apprehended of any; who is neither parviscient nor omniscient; neither parvipotent nor omnipotent; who has neither beginning nor end; immutable and indefectible—is the true entity All besides himself, the entire universe, is false, that is to say, is nothing whatsoever. Neither has it ever existed, nor does it now exist, nor will it exist at any time future."[2]

It is very interesting to note the likeness between Brahma thus portrayed and the 'Being' of Parmenides, who was the contemporary of Buddha and Confucius. "Being, he argued, is absolutely one. It is not an abstract unity, but the only reality. It is so that it alone is. Being, he further affirmed, is continuous and indivisible; it is everywhere like to itself, and everywhere alike present. Were there parts in being there would be plurality, and being would not be one—that is, would not be being. There can be no differences or distinctions in being; for what is different and distinct from being must be not-being, and not-being is not. . . . Being, he likewise held, is identical with thought. It could not otherwise be absolutely one. Thought, he said, is the same thing as being. Thought must be being; for being exists, and non-being is nothing." "His not-being did not mean non-existence, but all that sense and ordinary thought apprehend as existence; it included earth, air, ocean, and the minds of men."[3]

1 *Dialogues on Hindu Philosophy,* pp. 109, 123, and chaps. vii. and viii.

2 *Rational Refutation,* p. 176.

3 *Anti-Theistic Theories,* p. 353. Cf. also Lewes' *Hist. of Philosophy,* i. 56.

This 'being' is exactly the *sat, chit,* and *akhanda* of the Vedanta, whilst the idea of 'not-being' coincides entirely with the *vyavahariki* or *pratibhasiki satta.*

I

HAVING saluted my preceptor, who, from his having got rid of the notion of duality, is significantly named Adwayananda, I will now propound the essence of the Vedanta, according to my conception of it.

The Vedanta doctrine is based upon the Upanishads, and is likewise supported by the *Sariraka sutras* and other works.[1]

NOTES ON SECTION I

1. *Vedanta.*

This "literally signifies 'conclusion of the Veda,' and bears reference to the Upanishads, which are, for the most part, terminating sections of the Vedas to which they belong. It implies, however, *the doctrine* derived from them, and extends to books of sacred authority, in which that doctrine is thence deduced; and, in this large acceptation, it is the end and scope of the Vedas."[2]

2. *Sariraka sutras.*

This is a collection of aphorisms composed by Badarayana, and forms one of the six Darsanas or Systems of Philosophy. The word *sariraka* is said to be derived from the noun *sariraka,* which the commentator calls a contemptuous (*kutsita*) form of *sarira,* 'body' and means 'embodied' (scul). Sankaracharya's interpretation of these aphorisms and of the Upanishads, is the real authority for the tenets of the modern school.

Prior to the rise of Buddhism, dogma and ritual held undisputed sway. The followers of that heresy, however, presumed to appeal to reason, and their system was at once stigmatised as 'the since of reason' (*hetusastra*), which was then synonymous with heresy. This was doubtless the first systematic departure from the Mantras and Brahmanas; but the Brahmans were soon compelled to follow suit, and to them we owe the six so-called orthodox schools of Indian philosophy. I say 'so-called,' for the teaching of the Systems is no less a departure from the old religion than Buddhism is; but they profess respect for the Vedas, whilst the Buddhists openly repudiate them. The following remarks by an Indian scholar will be of interest here:

"In justice to the founders of our schools, we must confess that the opinions which they embodied in their systems had probably long been floating in the popular mind. The Buddhist defection had no doubt produced a spirit of scepticism from which the authors of the Sutras were not wholly free. And they, perhaps, laboured to give such a shape to those sceptical opinions as might be consistent with the supremacy of the Brahmanical order. Two things, they thought, were necessary for the maintenance of that supremacy—the toleration

1 Such as the Bhagavad-Gita, &c.

2 Colebrooke's *Essays,* I. 351.

of the Vedas and the substitution of metaphysical speculations for the too frequent performance of the Vedic ritual. Without the first, the foundation of Brahmanical supremacy would be cut away. Without the second, the Brahmanical mind would be doomed to a state of perpetual imbecility, familiar only with ceremonial observances, and utterly unable to meet the challenges put forth by sceptical heretics in the arena of controversy. Not that there was much essential difference in point of doctrine between the heretical and some of the orthodox schools. If Kapila could assert the non-existence of a Supreme Being, and if Kanada could attribute the primal action of eternal atoms to *adrishta,* I cannot see how there could be a marked difference of opinion between them and the heretics."[1]

The Bhagavad-Gita is accounted most orthodox, but this is what it says of the Vedas (ii. 42-46):—"A flowery doctrine, promising the reward of works performed in this embodied state, presenting numerous ceremonies, with a view to future gratification and glory, is prescribed by unlearned men, devoted to the injunctions of the Veda, assertors of its exclusive importance, lovers of enjoyment, and seekers after paradise. The restless minds of the men who, through this flowery doctrine, have become bereft of wisdom and are ardent in the pursuit of future gratification and glory, are not applied to contemplation. The Vedas have for their objects the three qualities; but be thou, Arjuna, free from these three qualities.... As great as is the use of a well which is surrounded on all sides by overflowing waters, so great [and no greater] is the use of the Vedas to a Brahman endowed with true knowledge."[2] King Asoka gave the death-blow to animal sacrifices in the third century before Christ, as various rock and pillar inscriptions bear witness; but the demolition of the rest of the fabric was effected by the orthodox philosophers, who spoke of it as "inferior science!"

3. *The Upanishads.*

These are short speculative treatises appended to the Vedas, and are about 235 in number.[3] Only thirteen of them, however, are really important or much quoted. They are the following:—*Rigveda:* Aitareya and Kausitaki. *Samaveda:* Kena and Chhandogya. *White Yajurveda:* Isa and Brihadaranyaka. *Black Yajurveda:* Katha, Maitri, Taittiriya, and Svetasvatara. *Atharvaveda:* Prasna, Mundaka, and Mandukya.

The word *Upanishad* is derived by Indian authors from the root *shad,* 'to destroy' (preceded by the prepositions *upa,* 'near,' and *ni,* 'down'), and is held to be that body of teaching which destroys illusion and reveals the Absolute. Max Muller, however, considers this explanation to be "wilfully perverse," and derives it from *sad,*

1 *Dialogues on Hindu Philosophy,* p. 73. For further discussion of this interesting question see Wilson's *Essays on the Religion of the Hindus,* ii. 85-87.

2 Muir's *Sanskrit Texts,* iii. 32.

3 *Hist. of Indian Literature,* p. 153 (*note*).

'to sit down,' "so that it would express the idea of session, or assembly of pupils sitting down near their teacher to listen to his instruction."[1] These tracts are thus described by E. B. Cowell:—"The Upanishads are usually in the form of dialogue; they are generally written in prose with occasional snatches of verse, but sometimes they are in verse altogether. They have no system or method; the authors are poets, who throw out their unconnected and often contradictory rhapsodies on the impulse of the moment, and have no thought of harmonizing to-day's feelings with those of yesterday or to-morrow. ... Through them all runs an unmistakable spirit of Pantheism, often in its most offensive form, as avowedly overriding all moral considerations; and it is this which has produced the general impression that the religion of the Veda is monotheistic."[2]

II

As this tract has for its subject the Vedanta, annd has clearly the same *praecognita*[3] as that system, it is unnecessary to consider them in detail. [But lest any one should not have read the large treatise, I may say that] the præcognita in that system are—

I. The qualified person (*adhikarin*).
II. The subject (*vishaya*).
III. The relation (*sambandha*).
VI. The purpose (*prayojana*).

1. *'The qualified person'* is one who possesses due intelligence; that is, one who, by reading the Vedas and Vedangas according to rule, either in this life or in a former one, has obtained a general idea of the meaning of the whole,—who, by performing the constant and occasional rites, the penances, and devotional exercises, and abstaining from things done with desire of reward and from those forbidden has got rid of all sin and so thoroughly cleansed his mind,—and who is possessed of the four means.

'The things done with desire of reward' (or 'optional things,' *kamya*) are the Jyotishtoma sacrifice and other things of a similar kind, which are the means of procuring heavèn and other desirable things.

The forbidden things, (*nishiddha*) are the slaying of a Brahman and the like, which result in hell and other undesirable things.

The 'constant rites' (*nitya*) are the Sàndhya prayers and the like, which cause ruin if left undone.

The 'occasional rites' (*naimittika*) are such as the birth-

1 *Sacred Books of the East,* vol. i. p. lxxx.
2 Elphinstone's *Hist. of India,* p. 282.
3 Ballantyne renders this by "moving considerations." The original is *anubandha.*

sacrifice following the birth of a son, and such like.

The 'penances' (*prayaschitta*) are such as the *Chandrayana* and others, which are used only for the removal of sin.

The 'devotional exercises' (*upasana*) are such as the system of Sandilya and the like, consisting of mental efforts directed towards Brahma with qualities.

The principal object of the constant and occasional rites and of the penances is the purification of the intellect; that of the devotional exercises is the concentration of the mind. As it is written in the Veda, "Him, the Self, Brahmans seek to know by means of the reading of the Veda and by sacrifice" (*Brihadaranyaka Upanishad*, 4. 4. 22); and in the Smriti, "By religious acts he destroys sin' (*Manu*, xii. 104).

An incidental results of the constant and occasional rites and of the devotional exercises is the acquisition of the abode of the progenitors and of the abode of Brahma; as the Veda says, "By works, the abode of the progenitors; by knowledge, the abode of the gods" (*Brihadaranyaka*, 1. 5. 16).

The 'four means' (*sadhana*) are (*a.*) discrimination between eternal and non-eternal substances, (*b.*) indifference to the enjoyment of rewards here and hereafter, (*c.*) the possession of quiescence, self-restraint, &c., and (*d.*) desire for release.

(*a.*) 'Discrimination between eternal and non-eternal substance, and that all else besides him is non-eternal.

(*b.*) 'Indifference to the enjoyment of rewards here or hereafter' is complete indifference to the enjoyment of the things of this life, such as garlands, sandals, and other objects of sense,—and of those pertaining to the next world, such as nectar and other sensuous objects,—because, being the result of works, they are non-eternal.

(*c.*) 'Quiescence, self-restraint, &c.,' are quiescence, self-restraint, abstinence, endurance, contemplative concentration, and faith.

'Quiescence' is the restraining of the mind from objects of sense opposed to hearing, &c.

'Self-restraint' is the turning away of the external organs from objects opposed to that hearing.

'Abstinence' is the continued abstaining of the external organs from sensuous objects opposed to that hearing, after they have been turned away from them; or it may be the abandonment of prescribed acts in a legitimate manner [*i.e.*, by becoming an ascetic].

'Endurance' is bearing the polarities of heat and cold, &c.

'Contemplative concentration' is the fixing of the restrained mind on hearing and such like things which are helpful to it.

'Faith' is belief in the utterances of the spiritual teacher and of the Vedanta.

(*d.*) 'Desire for release' is the longing for emancipation.

A man of this kind, the possessor of due intelligence, is '*a qualified person.*' As the Veda says, "The tranquil, restrained man, &c." (*Brihaddranyaka Upanishad*, 4. 4. 26); and as it is said elsewhere, "To the seeker of emancipation, who is tranquil in mind, who has subdued his senses, whose sins are gone, who is obedient and virtues, and who, long and continuously, has followed a teacher, is this to be taught" (*Upadesasahasri*, ver. 324).

II. '*The subject*' is the unity of souls and of Brahma, as pure intelligence, a fact which is to be demonstrated; for this is the purport of all Vedanta treatises.

III. '*The relation*' between that unity, the thing to be proved, and the proof derived from the Upanishads which set it forth, is that which is characterised as the condition of 'the explainer and thing to be explained.'

IV. '*The purpose*' is the removal of the ignorance regarding the unity which is to be demonstrated, and the acquisition of the joy which is the essence of Brahma. As the Veda says, "The knower of Self passes beyond sorrow" (*Chhandogya Upanishad*, 7. 1. 3); and again, "He who knows Brahma becomes Brahma" (*Mundaka*, 3. 2. 9).

As a man with a hot head goes to the water, so this qualified person, scorched by the fires of mundane existence, with its births, deaths, and other ills, takes a bundle of, firewood in his hands and approaches a spiritual teacher versed in the Vedas and intent upon Brahma, and becomes his follower. As it is said in the Veda, "In order to know Him, he should go with fuel in his hands to a teacher learned in the Vedas and intent on Brahma" (*Mundaka Upanishad*, 1. 2. 12). That teacher,[1] with great kindness, instructs him by the method of illusory attribution (*adhyaropa*), followed by its withdrawal (*apavada*). As it is written in the Veda, "To him, on drawing nigh with truly calmed mind and sense subdued, that learned one should[2] so expound, in truth, the Brahma lore, that he may know the true and undecaying Male" (*Mundaka*, 1. 2. 13).

1 In commenting on the foregoing passage, Sankaracharya lays stress on the need of a *teacher*, and says "*Sastrajno'pi svatantryena Brahmajnananveshanam na kuryat*," "Even though a man know the scriptures, he should not attempt to acquire the knowledge of Brahma independently." In *Panchadasi*, iv. 39-41, too, it is pointed out that, though at the *pralaya* duality will disappear of itself, yet deliverance from future births is not to be had without a previously acquired knowledge of Brahma, which knowledge it will be impossible to gain then, because there will be neither teacher nor scriptures!

2 *Provacha* is here equivalent to *prabrayat*, says Sankara.

NOTES ON SECTION II

1. The foregoing shows the compromise made by the philosophers with the pre-existing systems of ritual and devotion. They retained them, but merely, they said, as means of purifying the intellect for the reception of the higher truths,[1] a process similar to the polishing of a tarnished mirror so as to fit it to reflect an image.

"Whoever, therefore, hearing that the Vedantins believe in Brahma without qualities, infers that they reject Vishnu, Siva, and the rest of the pantheon, and that they discountenance idolatry and such things, and that they count the Puranas and similar writing false, labours under gross error."[2] In fact, it is laid down in *Panchadasi,* vi. 206-209, that any kind of god or demigod, or anything in the animal, vegetable, or mineral kingdom, may be properly worshipped as a portion of Iswara, and that such worship will bring a reward proportioned to the dignity of the object worshipped.

Worship is natural to man; and in making a compromise with the theologians the philosophers merely acknowledged this fact. Their system, however, like that of Buddha, had no object of worship, or indeed anything "to elicit and sustain a religious life;" so they were compelled "to crave the help of polytheism, and to treat the foullest orgies and cruellest rites of idolatry as acts of reasonable worship paid indirectly to the sole and supreme Being.'[3]

It is laid down, however, in *Panchadasi,* iv. 43-46, that as soon as the knowledge of the truth is obtained, the sacred writings themselves, as a portion of the unreal dualism, are to be abandoned, just as a torch is extinguished when one has no further need of it, or as the husk is thrown away by one who merely wants the grain! The dishonesty of Pantheism is thus clearly seen. For "if it look upon the popular deities as mere fictions of the popular mind, its association with polytheism can only mean a conscious alliance with falsehood, the deliberate propagation of lies. If, on the other hand, it regard them as really manifestations of the Absolute Being, it must believe this on the authority of revelation or tradition,"[4] the whole of which the Vedantist classes with unrealities!

2. *'In this life or in a former one.'*

It is this tenet of a succession of births that furnishes the *raison d'etre* of the systems of philosophy, as their professed aim is to provide a way of deliverence from them. The doctrine of metempsychosis still prevails in India, Ceylon, Burma, Tibet, Tartary, and China, and is accepted, therefore, by the larger portion of the human race. It would be a source of much satisfaction to us if we could discover the time and place of its birth. It was not held by the Aryan family or by the early Indian settlers, for the Vedas recognise the continued existence of the soul after death in some heavenly sphere, and contain no distinct reference whatever to the fact of transmigration.[5] Its first appearance in orthodox writings is in

1 Cf. *Mundaka Upanishad,* 3. 1. 5.
2 *Rational Refutation,* p. 195.
3 *Anti-Theistic Theories,* p. 389.
4 *Anti-Theistic Theories,* p. 390.
5 Wilson's *Essays on Sanskrit Literature,* iii. 345.

the Chhandogya and Brihadaranyaka Upanishads, which are believed by A. Weber to have been composed at about the same period, the former in the west of Hindustan, the latter in the east. He, however, refers them to a "comparatively recent date," and tells us that the doctrines promulgated in the latter by Yajnavalkya are "completely Buddhistic."[1] That being the case, we may justly consider these two treatises to have been post-Buddhistic; and there then remains no ancient orthodox composition which can claim to have set forth the doctrine of transmigration prior to the appearance of Buddha. It is embodied, it is true, in Manu's Code of Laws, for which a very high antiquity has been claimed; but there can be no reasonable doubt that the present redaction of it was posterior to the rise of Buddhism, and some would even bring it down to as late a time as the third century before Christ.[2] But even if it be true that the doctrine was first publicly taught by Buddha, it by no means follows that he was the originator of it, and that it had not been a matter of speculation long before his time. As a matter of fact, the theory of the transmignation of *soul* was assuredly not his, for he totally denied the existence of soul. What he taught was the transmigration of *karma*, that is, of the aggregate of all a man's actions in every state of existence in which he has lived.[3] According to him, a man is made up of five aggregates (Sanskrit, *skandha;* Pali, *khanda*) of properties or qualities, viz., 1. *Rupa,* organised body, comprising twenty-eight divisions; 2. *Vedana,* sensation, comprising eighteen divisions; 3. *Sanjna,* perception, comprising six divisions; 4. *Sanskara,* discrimination, comprising fifty-two divisions; and 5. *Vijnana,* consciousness, comprising eighty-nine divisions. At death, these five are broken up and dispersed, never to be re-united. But, besides *karma,* there is another property inherent in all sentient beings, named *upadana,* or 'cleaving to existing objects;' and these two survive the dispersion of the aggregates and produce a new being. "By *upadana* a new existence is produced, but then means of its operation is controlled by the *karma* with which it is connected. It would sometimes appear that *upadana* is the efficient cause of reproduction, and that at other times it is *karma.* But in all cases it is the *karma* that appoints whether the being to be produced shall be an insect in the sunbeam, a worm in the earth, a fish in the sea, a fowl in the air, a beast in the forest, a man, a restless *dewa* or *brahma* of the celestial world.'[4]

Such is the Buddhist notion of transmigration; and it would be more reasonable to suppose it to have been an adaptation of the usual theory than to regard the latter as modified from it.

The other Asiatic countries named above obtained the doctrine, together with the rest of Buddhism, from India, and can therefore give us no help in our search. Turning to Europe, we find the

1 *History of Indian Literature,* pp. 71, 73, 285.

2 Elphinstone's *History of India,* 6th ed., by Cowell, p. 249. The most probable date of the death of Buddha is 477 B.C.

3 Hardy's *Legends and Theories of the Buddhists,* p. 164.

4 Hardy's *Manual of Buddhism,* p. 409.

metempsychosis amongst the philosophy of Pythagoras, who is supposed to have been born some time between 604 and 520 B.C.[1] His life is "shrouded in the dim magnificence of legends," amongst which we should doubtless class the theory of his having visited India. Still the similarity of much of his system to that of Indian philosophers is very curious, and Colebrooke thought that it was borrowed from them.

With regard, however, to the supposed Eastern origin of much of that philosopher's teaching, George Henry Lewes thus wrote: "Every dogma in it has been traced to some prior philosophy. Not a vestige will remain to be called the property of the teacher himself if we restore to the Jews, Indians, Egyptians, Chaldeans, Phœnicians, nay, even Thracians, those various portions which he is declared to have borrowed from them. All this pretended plagiarism we incline to think extremely improbable. Pythagoras was a successor of Anaximander, and his doctrines, in so far as we can gather their leading tendency, were but a continuation of that abstract and deductive philosophy of which Anaximander was the originator."[2]

But this by no means exhausts the field for inquiry, for Egypt is known to have held the theory of transmigration, possibly before it was taught in Greece; but whether it was introduced from without, or evolved from the inner consciousness of the nation itself, we cannot determine. We have to acknowledge ourselves completely baffled, then, in our search for the birthplace of this important dogma; and whether it originated in the West or in the East, or arose simultaneously in both worlds, it is absolutely impossible to say, and we must be content to leave the question in the thick haze which impenetrably enshrouds it.

3. *'Reading the Veda,'* &c.

The study of the Veda and the practice of its ritual being prerequisites to the initiation into the higher mysteries, the advantages offered by philosophy were beyond the reach of the masses, and for them something simpler and more attractive was provided. But the real object of the provision thus made, whether for the learned or the ignorant, for the few or the many, was to put forth a counter-attraction to the system of Sakya Muni.

When we think of the wonderful deliverance that had been offered by Buddhism to the priest-ridden communities of India, of the vast number of the adherents, and of its great power, which so effectually checked Brahman supremacy for centuries, it seems almost incredible that it should ever have succumbed, and have been driven beyond the Himalayas. Yet so it was. Possibly its very success engendered indolence and inactivity on the part of those who ought actively to have maintained and propagated it;[3] or its extreme simplicity and strict morality may at length have proved irksome and rendered it

1 Buddha is supposed to have lived eighty years, and so was probably born about 557 B.C. Hardy's *Manual of Buddhism,* p. 366.

2 *History of Philosophy, 4th edition,* i. 26.

3 Wilson's *Essays on the Religion of the Hindus,* ii. 367.

unpopular;[1] or the weakness necessarily inherent in a religion without a God to be loved and worshipped may have been at length manifested in it, and so have opened the way for the astute Brahmans, who were ever on the watch for opportunities for recovering their long-lost sway. But be this as it may, the opportunity came, and the means employed for eradicating the heresy were twofold, namely, persecution and the introduction of a sensuous and attractive worship.

The former is supposed to have been commenced as early as the third century of our era, but to have been actively and more successfully carried on during the fifth and sixth centuries. The probability of the persecution of the latter period is remarkably strengthened by the fact that Buddhism received a fresh impulse in China in A.D. 519, was introduced into the Korea in A.D. 530, in Japan in A.D. 540-550, and into Java during the sixth and seventh centuries, which witnessed the arrival of large numbers of Hindu emigrants.[2] We have evidence of the fact of the decline of Buddhism in those early centuries from the diary of the Chinese pilgrim Hiouen Thsang, who came to India in the year 629 A.D. to study original Buddhist works, and during his residence of fourteen or fifteen years travelled over a great part of the country.

He found large numbers of flourishing monasteries, conspicuous amongst which was that of Nalanda (north-east of Gaya), which contained 10,000 resident monks, some of whom were "visitors from all parts of India, who had come to study the abstruser Buddhist books under its renowned teachers;" but on the other hand, there were vast numbers deserted and in ruins, whilst Hindu temples abounded and 'heretics' swarmed in every city.[3]

The struggle was renewed, at the end of the seventh century, by the famous Mimansaka, Kumarila Bhatta, who was regarded as "an incarnation of Kartikeya, the object of whose descent was the extirpation of the Saugatas" (Buddhists), and ended in the complete expulsion of the latter from the Dekhan. The great controversialist Sankaracharya, too, who lived a century later, is supposed by some to have used sterner weapons than the pen in demolishing heretics; but, on the other hand, his "mild character" and "uniformly gentle and tolerant" disposition, as well as the absence from his writings of all mention of the persecution of his opponents, have been brought forward in disproof of the charge.[4] Notwithstanding the efforts of their enemies to uproot them, the Buddhists were still found on the Coromandel Coast in the eighth and ninth centuries, and in Guzerat, and on the throne of Bengal in the twelfth century; but after that they were heard of no more. In the fourteenth century they were not found south of Kashmir, and by the sixteenth century they appear to have been rarely met with even there.[5]

The attempt to suppress Buddhism by fire and sword was supple-

1 Weber's *History of Indian Literature,* p. 289 (*note*).
2 Wilson's *Essays on Sanskrit Literature,* iii. 198.
3 Elphinstone's *History of India,* 6th ed., by Cowell, pp. 288-299.
4 *Essays on Sanskrit Literature,* iii. 191-197.
5 *Ibid.,* p. 225.

mented, however, by other measures, in order to place reviving Brahmanical supremacy on a firm basis. These, somewhat after the fashion of Balaam's tactics for the seduction and ruin of Israel, consisted of the introduction of an extremely sensuous... form of Krishna-worship, together with the cults of certain female deities.[1] "The Brahmans saw, on regaining their supremacy after the fall of the rival school, that it would be impossible to enlist the popular sympathy in their favour without some concessions to the Sudras. They accordingly pitched on the well-known, and perhaps already deified, character of Krishna, and set it up as an object of universal worship. And in order to make it the more fascinating to the popular mind, and to give that mind a strong impulse in a direction the very opposite of Buddhism, they invested their new god with those infirmities of the flesh from which Sakya Muni is said to have been somewhat unnaturally free.[2] .....

The time of the introduction of Krishna-worship having, however, formed a subject of debate amongst scholars, it may be well to dwell upon it further. It should be stated at the outset that there is an important difference between the mere deification of Krishna and his elevation to the rank of supreme deity... References to the first, that is, to his apotheosis, have been found by Professor Bhandarkar in the Mahabhashya, which he assigns to the second century before Christ;[3] but the latter, the Krishna-cultus proper, according to Weber, is not found before the fifth or sixth century of our era;[4] and its best authority, the Bhagavata Purana (book x.), is ascribed by Colebrooke and "many learned Hindus" to the twelfth century.[5]

1 Weber's *History of Indian Literature,* p. 289 (*note*).

2 K. M. Banerjea's *Dialogues on the Hindu Philosophy,* p. 520. In *Bhagavad Gita,* iv. 8, Krishna is made to speak of himself as appearing in every age for the complete deliverance of the saintly, the overthrow of the wicked, and the establishment of righteousness; and in xviii. 66 as the deliverer from all sin! The Bhagavata Purana is said to have been related by the Sage Suka to King Parikshit, who, after listening to the account of Krishna's sports, is said to have inquired how it was that he who became incarnate "for the establishment of virtue" and the repression of vice, and who was "the expounder, author, and guardian of the bulwarks of righteousness," could indulge in such sports. The reply to this very proper question was as follows:—"The transgression of virtue and the daring acts which are witnessed in superior beings (*Isvaranam*) must not be charged as faults to these glorious persons. ... Let no one other than a superior being ever even in thought practise the same. ... The word of superior beings is true, and so also their conduct is sometimes [correct]: let a wise man observe their command, which is right. ... Since Munis are uncontrolled and act as they please, how can there be any restraint upon him (the Supreme Deity) when he has voluntarily assumed a body?" "This passage is followed by an assurance on the part of the author of the Purana that the person who listens with faith to the narrative of Krishna's sports with the cowherd's wives, and who repeats it to others, shall attain to strong devotion to that deity, and shall speedily be freed from love." —*Muir's Sanskrit Texts,* iv. 50 f. *Bhagavata Purana,* x. 33, 27-40.

3 *Indian Antiquary,* ii. 60.

4 *Ibid.,* p. 285.

5 *Miscellaneous Essays,* i. 94.

In the Gopalatapani Upanishad, too, we find Krishna, "the beloved of the *gopis,*" set forth as the supreme deity; but this work is justly supposed by Weber to be very modern,[1] and Colebrooke regarded its claim to antiquity as "particularly suspicious." His remarks on this whole question are worthy of attention. He says: "Although the *Ramatapaniya* be inserted in all the collections of Upanishads which I have seen; and the *Gopalatápaniya* appear in some, yet I am inclined to doubt their genuineness, and to suspect that they have been written in times modern when compared with the remainder of the Vedas. This suspicion is chiefly grounded on the opinion that the sects which now worship Rama and Krishna as incarnations of Vishnu are comparatively new. I have not found in any other part of the Vedas the least trace of such a worship. ... According to the notions which I entertain of the real history of the Hindu religion, the worship of Rama and of Krishna by the *Vaishnavas,* and that of Mahadeva and Bhavani by the *Saivas* and *Saktas,* have been generally introduced since the persecution of the *Bauddhas* and *Jainas.* ... The overthrow of the sect of Buddha in India has not effected the full revival of the religious system inculcated in the Vedas. Most of what is there taught is now obsolate, and, in its stead, new orders of religious devotees have been instituted, and new forms of religious ceremonies have been established. Rituals founded on the *Puranas* and observances borrowed from another source, the *Tantras,* have, in a great measure, antiquated the institutions of the Vedas. In particular, the sacrificing of animals before the idols of Kali has superseded the less sanguinary practice of the *Yajna;* and the adoration of Rama and of Krishna has succeeded to that of the elements and planets. If this opinion be well founded, it follows that the Upanishads in question have probably been composed in later times, since the introduction of those sects which hold Rama and Gopala in peculiar veneration."[2]

The date of that most important treatise the Bhagavad Gita, in which Krishna is regarded as the Supreme, has not been determined. On account of remarkable resemblances in it to some of the ideas and expressions of the Bible, Lorinser, writing in 1869, asserted that it was probably indebted to the latter for them. He was of opinion that the Brahmanas borrowed Christian ideas from the early Christian communities in India and applied them to Krishna.[3] The existence of a Christian Church in India in the first or second century, as maintained by Lorinser, has not, however, been satisfactorily established. According to Burnell, "the Manichæan mission to India in the third century A.D. is the only historical fact that we know of in relation to Christian mission in India before we get as low as the sixth century."[4] However this may be, the sudden appearance on the Hindu horizon of *bhakti,* as distinguished from the older *sraddha,*[5]

1 *History of Indian Literature,* p. 169.
2 *Miscellaneous Essays,* i. 99-101.
3 *Indian Antiquary,* ii. 283.
4 *Ibid.,* iv. 182.
5 Cowell's *Aphorisms of Sandilya,* p. viii.

is a fact the explanation of which is almost impossible if a previous contact with Christianity is denied.

Lorinser's position has been vehemently assailed by Kashinath Telang of Bombay, but not, in my opinion, with complete success. It has been disputed, too, by P. Windisch of Heidelberg, who, while admitting that "some surprising parallel passages" have been adduced, considers "the immediate introduction of the Bible into the explanation of the Bhagavad Gita" to be permature.[1]

Weber regards Lorinser's attempt as "overdone," but adds that "he is not in principle opposed to the idea which that writer maintains."[2] Indeed this eminent scholar has declared his own belief in the indebtedness of the Krishna-cult to Christianity, as the following quotation will show: "(1.) The reciprocal action and mutual influence of gnostic and Indian conceptions in the first centuries of the Christian era are evident, however difficult it may be at present to say what in each is peculiar to it or borrowed from the other. (2.) The worship of Krishna as sole god is one of the latest phases of Indian religious systems, of which there is no trace in Varahamihira, who mentions Krishna, but only in passing. (3.) This worship of Krishna as sole god has no intelligible connection with his earlier position in the Brahmanical legends. There is a gap between the two, which apparently nothing but the supposition of an external influence can account for. (4.) The legend in the *Mahabharata* of Svetädwipa, and the revelation which is made there to Narada by Bhagavat himself, shows that Indian tradition bore testimony to such an influence. (5.) The legends of Krishna's birth, the solemn celebration of his birthday, in the honours of which his mother, Devaki, participates, and finally his life as a herdsman, a phase the furthest removed from the original representation, can only be explained by the influence of Christian legends, which, received one after the other by individual Indians in Christian lands, were modified to suit their own ways of thought, and may also have been affected by the labours of individual Christian teachers down to the latest times."[3]

The Mahabharata, in which the Gita lies imbedded, is the work of "widely distant periods;" and though some portion of it is said to have existed in Patanjali's time,[4] that is, in the second century before Christ, its present redaction was probably not complete until "some centuries after the commencement of our era."[5] Chronology, therefore, furnishes no disproof of the theory advanced above as to the origin of Krishna-worship.

4. *'The Jyotishtoma sacrifice.'*

This appears to have been a cycle of seven sacrifices, of which one called Agnishtoma was the first. Haug says that in many places the term Jyotishtoma is equivalent to Agnishtoma, which is the model

1 *Indian Antiquary,* iv. 79. 2 *Ibid.*
3 *Indian Antiquary,* ii. 285. 4 *Ibid.*, i. 350.
5 Weber's *History of Indian Literature,* p. 188; and Muir's *Sanskrit Texts,* iv. 169.

of all Soma sacrifices of one day's duration. The ceremonies connected with the Agnishtoma sacrifice lasted for five days, but those of the first four days were merely introductory to the crowning rites of the last day, on which the squeezing, offering, and drinking of the Soma juice took place at the morning, midday, and evening libations. The Soma ceremony is said to have been the holiest rite in the whole Brahmanical service.[1]

5. *'The slaying of a Brahman.'*

There are numerous references in Manu's code to the awfulness of this crime; and the consequences of even a comman assault on his sacred person are something terrific. The following are examples:

"That twice-born man who merely assaults a Brahman with intent to hurt, wanders about in the hell called *Tamisra* for a hundred years; whilst he who 'of malice aforethought' strikes him, even with a blade of grass, goes through twenty-one different births of a low order" (*Manu,* iv. 165, 166).

"A king should never slay a Brahman, though convicted of every crime under the sun; he should expel him from the country, unharmed, with all his property. There is no greater crime in the world than the slaughter of a Brahman; a king, therefore, should not even contemplate it with his mind" (vii. 380, 381).

"The (unintentional) slayer of a Brahman should make a hut for himself in the forest, and dwell there for twelve years for purification, living on alms, and having the head of his victim set up as a banner" (xi. 72).

"He who, with murderous intent, merely threatens a Brahman with a stick goes to hell for a hundred years; whilst he who actually strikes him goes for a thousand years" (xi. 206).

6. *'The Sandhya prayers.'*

"Let him daily, after rinsing his mouth, observe the two Sandhyas, repeating the Savitri in a pure place according to rule" (*Manu,* ii. 222).

Colebrooke says: "The duty of bathing in the morning and at noon, if the man be a householder, and in the evening also, if he belong to an order of devotion, is inculcated by pronouncing the strict observance of it no less efficacious than a rigid penance in expiating sins, especially the early bath in the months of Magha, Phalguna, Kartika; and the bath being particularly enjoined as a salutary ablution, he is permitted to bathe in his own house, but without prayers, if the weather or his own infirmities prevent his going forth; or he may abridge the ceremonies and use fewer prayers if a religious duty or urgent business require his early attendance. The regular bath consists of ablutions followed by worship and by the inaudible recitation of the Gayatri with the names of the worlds."[2] The sacred Gayatri or Savitri is this: *'Tat savitur varenyam bhargo devasya dhimahi dhiyo yo nah prachodayat,'* which Colebrooke thus translates:

1 See Haug's *Aitareya Brahmana,* i. 59-63, ii. 240.

2 *Miscellaneous Essays,* i. 142.

"Let us meditate on the adorable light of the divine ruler (Savitri); may it guide our intellects."

7. *'The Chandrayana.'*

This, to quote from Monier Williams' Dictionary, is "a religious observance or expiatory penance regulated by the moon's age. In consists in diminishing the daily consumption of food every day by one mouthful for the dark half of the month, beginning with fifteen at the full moon until the quantity is reduced to zero at the new moon, and then increasing it in like manner during the fortnight of the moon's increase." This kind is called by Manu (xi. 216, Scholium), *Pipilikamadhya,* 'that which has the middle thin like an ant.' If, however, the rite commences at the new moon, and goes from zero up to fifteen and then decreases again, it is called *Yavamadhya,* 'that which is thick in the middle like a barley-corn' (xi. 217). There are two other varieties called *Yati* and *Sisu.* The former consists of eating eight mouthfuls a day at midday and fasting during the morning and evening for a whole month; the latter, of eating four mouthfuls in the morning and four in the evening every day for a month. A fifth variety, which appears to have no name, consists of eating 240 mouthfuls during the month, to be divided into daily portions at the will of the eater. Thus, as the Scholiast says, he may one day eat ten mouthfuls, another five, another sixteen, and another none at all, and so on (xi. 218-220).

8. *'The system of Sandilya'* (*Sandilyavidya*).

What this was is not known. It was clearly not the doctrine of faith which is set forth in the Sandilya aphorisms. See preface to Cowell's translation of the latter.

9. *'Longing for emancipation.'*

The idea of *mukti* is not found in the first two divisions of the Veda, and the Svetasvatara is the only Upanishad in which it is fully and unmistakably developed. "The Brahmans had certainly been pondering it for some time before the rise of Buddhism. It was probably they themselves who instilled it into the mind of Sakya. It was perhaps their own aspiration after something better than the degrading pleasures of Indra's territories that first suggested the futility of rites and ceremonies to the fertile imagination of the young prince of Kapilavastu. But it was the prince himself who appears to have imparted a coherent shape to the doctrine, which, in some of the pre-Buddhistic Upanishads, appears in a chaotic state of disconnected fragments, not unfrequently by the side of the very contrary idea of sensuous enjoyments. Sakya appears to have first separated the two by contending that rites and ceremonies do not contribute to our highest good, and that it was *nirvana*[1] alone which could secure our final escape from the miseries of sensuous life. In post-Buddhistic writings the notion of emancipation which pervades the philosophy of the Nyaya, the Sankhya, and the Vedanta, appears in a consistent

1 See this explained in Childers' *Pali Dictionary,* s.v. *Nibbanam.*

form as distinct from that of heavenly enjoyment. *Swarga* and *apawarga* are always contrasted."[1]

10. *'The qualified person.'*

The text shows that in order to qualify for initiation into the esoteric doctrines, the aspirant had to go through a long preparatory course. It may be interesting to compare with it that which the pupils of Pythagoras were required to pass through before receiving instruction in his wisdom. "For five years the novice was condemned to silence. Many relinquished the task in despair; they were unworthy of the contemplation of pure wisdom. Others, in whom the tendency to loquacity was observed to be less, had the period commuted. Various humiliations had to be endured; various experiments were made of their powers of self-denial. By these Pythagoras judged whether they were worldly-minded, or whether they were fit to be admitted into the sanctuary of science. Having purged their souls of the baser particles by purifications, sacrifices, and initiations, they were admitted to the sanctuary, where the higher part of the soul was purged by the knowledge of truth, with consists in the knowledge of immaterial and eternal things."[2]

11. *'Illusory attribution &c.'* (*adhyaropapavada*).

In order to describe the pure abstraction Brahma, the teacher attributes to him, or superimposes on him, certain qualities which in reality do not belong to him, and then afterwards withdrawing them, teaches that the residuum is the undifferenced Absolute.

"When the Vedantins speak of the origin of the world, they do not believe its origin to be true. This mode of expression they call false imputation (*adhyaropa*). It consists in holding for true that which is false, in accommodation to the intelligence of the uninitiated. At a further stage of instruction, when the time has arrived for propounding the esoteric view, the false imputation is gainsaid, and this gainsaying is termed rescission[3] (*apavada*)."

12. I will conclude the notes on this section with the following extract: "If these rules of initiation be truthful, then the doctrine of one being is necessarily falsified, for they presuppose the existence of the *guru* and of all things which are necessary for the performance of the Vedic ritual; and it the rules are themselves illusory, the Vedantic initiation must itself be an illusion; and if the initiation be false, the indoctrination must be false too; for he only gets knowledge who has got an *acharya*. The Vedanta will not allow that its grand consummation can be brought about without a qualified tutor. If there be no *acharya*, there can be no teaching; and if the indoctrination is a delusion, the conclusion of this spiritual exercise, *i.e.*, *mukti*, must be the grandest of delusions; and the whole system of Vedantism, all its texts and sayings, its precepts and promises, its *acharya* and *adhikari*,

1 *Dialogues on Hindu Philosophy*, p. 325. See also Wilson's *Works*, ii. 113.

2 Lewes' *History of Philosophy*, i. 22.

3 *Rational Refutation*, p. 209.

are therefore built like a house (as Ramanuja suggests) upon an imaginary mathematical line."[1]

III

ILLUSORY attribution is the attributing to the real of that which is unreal; as a snake is imagined in a rope which is not a snake.

The *'real'* is Brahma, existent, intelligence, and joy, without a second. The *'unreal'* is the whole mass of unintelligent things, beginning with ignorance.

'Ignorance,' they say, is something not describable as existent or non-existent, an entity, composed of the three qualities, antagonistic to knowledge.

[Its existence is established] by one's own consciousness of being ignorant, and also by the Veda, [which speaks of it as] "the own power of God, concealed by its emanations"[2] (*Svetasvatara Upanishad,* i. 3).

NOTES ON SECTION III

1. *'The real'* (*vastu*).

The characteristics of Brahma have already been considered in the opening notes, and it is in accordance with the doctrine of existences, as there explained, that Brahma is here declared to be the only reality. All else is 'unreal' (*avastu*), and imagined by ignorance. This is plainly put in the *Adhyatma-Ramayana* (p. 477): "The entire universe, movable and immovable, comprising bodies, intellects, and the organs, everything that is seen or heard, from Brahma down to a tuft of grass, is that which is called Matter (*prakriti*), is that which is known as Illusion."

The phenomenal is got rid of in this simple way, by quietly ignoring the evidence of the senses; but the non-duality thus established is purely imaginary. For "even appearances or illusions are phenomena which require to be explained, and they cannot be explained on the hypothesis of absolute unity. They imply that besides the absolute being there are *minds* which can be haunted by appearances, and which can be deluded into believing that these appearances are realities."[3]

It has been already stated that the teaching of the earlier Upanishads was a *parinamavada,* not a *mayavada or vivarttavada.* Whence, then, did this theory of the unreality of all things arise? The most probable answer is, that it was adopted from the Buddhists, the great supporters of Idealism. This was the opinion of Vijnana Bhikshu, the learned commentator on the Sankhya philosophy, who flourished about 300 years ago,[4] and who wrote of the "quasi-Vedantins" of his time as "upstart disguised Buddhists, advocates of the theory of Maya,"

1 *Dialogues on Hindu Philosophy,* p. 421.

2 Literally, 'by its qualities,' which Sankaracharya says means "by earth, &c., which are the products of matter" (*svagunaih prakriti-karyabhutaih prithivyadibhih*).

3 *Anti-Theistic Theories,* p. 419.

4 Preface to Hall's *Sankhya Sara,* p. 37 (*note*).

and quoted a passage from the Padma Purana[1] where the doctrine of Maya is also stigmatised as nothing but disguised Buddhism.[2] The Svetasvatara is said to be the only Upanishad in which the illusory nature of phenomena is plainly taught, and that tract is evidently post-Buddhistic. In the preface to his translation of it, Dr. Roer says that it "does not belong to the series of the more ancient Upanishads, or of those which preceded the foundation of the philosophical systems; for it shows, in many passages, an acquaintance with them, introduces the Vedanta, Sankhya, and Yoga by their very names—mentions the reputed founder of the Sankhya, Kapila, and appears even to refer to doctrines which have been always considered as heterodox. . . . As the mythological views of the Svetasvatara are those of a later time, when the worship of Siva and of the divine Saktis or energies had gained ground, in contradistinction to the ancient Upanishads, where only the gods of the Vedas are introduced, so also its philosophical doctrine refers to a more modern period." In his opinion, it was composed not very long before the time of Sankaracharya, who is thought to have flourished in the eighth century of our era.[3]

2. *'Ignorance'* (*ajnana*).

This is synonymous with Nescience (*avidya*) and Illusion (*maya*), and though called the material cause of the universe, nevertheless heads the list of unrealities! Indeed it has been said that "the tenet of the falseness of Ignorance is the very keystone of the Vedanta!"[4] Its properties are the following:

(a.) *'Not describable as existent or non-existent.'*

If allowed to have true existence, dualism of cause ensues; and if it be said to be non-existent, it falls into the same category as a hare's horn, the son of a barren woman, and such like absolute nonentitles, and no causation could then be attributed to it. So, to avoid the dilemma, it is said to be neither the one nor the other. Howbeit it is acknowledged to have a practical existence, and to have been eternally associated with Brahma;[5] and, as a matter of fact, Brahma and Maya are the exact counterpart of the Purusha and Prakriti of the Sankhya, which is a professedly dualistic system.

An Indian writer speaks of Illusion as "the inscrutable principle regulating the universe of phenomena, or rather the world itself regarded as ultimately inconceivable;[6] and, elsewhere, as "the mystery by which the absolute Brahma brings himself into relation to the universe;[7] but he allows that, after all, this is rather a confes-

1 This work is supposed by Professor H. H. Wilson to have been composed, in part, in the twelfth century. *Vishnu Purana,* vol. i. p. xxxiv.

2 *Dialogues on Hindu Philosophy,* pp. 309-313. *Sankhya-pravachanabhashya,* p. 29.

3 Colebrooke's *Essays,* i. 357. 4 *Rational Refutation,* p. 193.

5 *Ibid.,* p. 35 (*note*).

6 *The Pandit* (*new series*), iii. 506.

7 *Journal of R. A. S.* (*new series*), x. 38.

sion of the mystery than a solution of it. By Sankaracharya it is defined as "the aggregate of all powers, causes, and effects." But a principle or power producing such palpable results as the universe, &c., must have a very real existence, however 'inscrutable' it may be; and the definition of the text is absolute nonsense. The philosopher Kapila discusses this point in some of the aphorisms of his first book: "Not from Ignorance too [does the soul's bondage, as the Vedantists hold, arise], because that which is not a reality is not adapted to binding. If it [Ignorance] *be* [asserted by you to be] a reality, then there is an abondonment of the [Vedantic] tenet. And [if you assume Ignorance to be a reality, then] there would be a *duality* through [there being] something of a different kind [from soul,—which you asserters of *non-duality* cannot contemplate allowing]. If [the Vedantin alleges, regarding Ignorance, that] it is in the shape of both these opposites, [we say] no, because no such thing is known [as is at once real and unreal]. [Possibly the Vedantin may remonstrate], '*We* are not asserters of any six categories like the Vaiseshikas and others [—like the Vaiseshikas who arrange all things under six heads, and the Naiyayikas who arrange them under sixteen; —'therefore we hold that there *is* such a thing as Ignorance, which is at once real and unreal, or (if you prefer it) which differs at once from the real and unreal, because this is established by proofs,' scriptural or otherwise, which are satisfactory to *us*, although they may not comply with all the technical requisitions of Gautama's scheme of argumentative exposition. To which we reply], Even although this be not compulsory [that the eategories be reckoned six or sixteen], there is no acceptance of the inconsistent, else we come to the level of children, madmen, and the like."[1]

(b.) *'An entity'* (*bhavarupa*).

This is laid down in opposition to the notion of the logicians that *ajnana,* 'not-knowledge,' is merely the equivalent of *jnanabhava,* 'absence of knowledge.'

(c.) *'Antagonistic to knowledge'* (*jnanavirodhi*).

This may possibly mean, 'whose foe is knowledge,' that is, 'which is capable of being destroyed by knowledge.' A man might argue, says the commentator, that Ignorance being, according to the Veda, 'unborn,' spread out everywhere like the ether, and having the semblance of reality, deliverance from its power and from transmigration is impossible; but it is not so, for notwithstanding the power of Ignorance, it nevertheless yields to the cognition of Brahma, as the darkness flees before the light. There can be no doubt, from what has been so far asserted of Ignorance, that the logicians have rightly defined it as 'absence of apprehension,' and that it is also 'misapprehension.' For further on we shall find two powers attributed to Ignorance, namely, those of 'concealment' (*avarana*) and 'protection' (*vikshepa*), which are nothing else than 'absence of apprehension,' and 'misapprehension,' respectively.[2]

[1] *Sankhya Aphorisms*, translated by Dr. Ballantyne, pp. 6-8.
[2] *Rational Refutation*, p. 248.

(d.) *'Composed of the three quantities'* (*trigunatmaka*).

This is stated, too, in Bhagavad Gita, vii. 14: "Inasmuch as this divine Maya of mine, composed of the qualities, is hard to be surmounted, none but those who resort to me cross over it." The *Prakriti,* that is, 'Nature' or 'matter,' of the Sankhya has been thus described:—"Nature is unintelligent substance, and is the material cause of the world. It consists of goodness, passion, and darkness in equal proportions. And here it should be borne in mind that it is not the goodness, passion, and darkness, popularly reckoned qualities of particular states of the soul, that are intended in the Sankhya. In it they are *unintelligent substances.* Otherwise, how could they be the material cause of earth and like gross things?"[1]

Every word of this applies to the Vedantic 'Ignorance' or 'Illusion,' which in the Svetasvatara Upanishad (iv. 10) is called Prakriti, or matter, and which is held to be the material cause of the world.

How this fact is to be reconciled with the previous portions of the definition is for the Vedantist to explain, if he can!

IV

THIS Ignorance is treated as one or as many, according as it is regarded as a collective or distributive aggregate. Just as, when regarding a collection of trees as a whole, we speak of them as one thing, namely, a forest; or as, when regarding a collection of waters as a whole we call them a lake, so when we look at the aggregate of the ignorances residing in individual souls and seeming to be manifold, we regard them as one. As it is said in the Veda, "[The one, unborn, individual soul, approaches] the one, unborn (Nature)" (*Svetasvatara Upanishad,* iv. 5).

This collective aggregate [of Ignorances], having as its associate that which is most excellent,[2] abounds in pure goodness. Intelligence[3] associated with it, having the qualities of omniscience, omnipotence, and universal control, real and unreal, imperceptible, the internal ruler and the cause of the world, is called Iswara.

Omniscience is attributed to him as the illuminator of the whole of Ignorance. As the Veda says, "Who knows all [generally], who knows everything [particularly]" (*Mundaka,* i. 1, 9).

This totality [of Ignorance], being the cause of all things, is Iswara's causal body. It is also called 'the sheath of bliss,' because it is replete with bliss, and envelops all things like a sheath; and 'dreamless sleep,' because everything reposes in

1 *Rational Refutation,* p. 42.

2 Namely, the *whole* of that portion of Brahma which is associated with ignorance.

3 *Chaitanya* or *Brahma.*

it,—on which account it is also regarded as the scene of the dissolution of all subtile and gross bodies.

As, when regarding a forest as a distributive aggregate composed of trees, there is a perception of its manifoldness, which is also perceived in the case of a lake regarded as a distributive aggregate of waters,—so, when viewing Ignorance distributively, we perceive it to be multiplex. As the Veda says, "Indra, by his supernatural powers, appears multiform" (*Rig-Veda*, 6. 47. 18).

Thus, then, a thing is regarded as a collective or distributive aggregate according as it is viewed as a whole or as a collection of parts.

Distributive ignorance, having a humble[1] associate, abounds in impure goodness. Intelligence associated with it, having the qualities of parviscience and parvipotence, is called *Prajna*.[2] The smallness of its intelligence is owing to its being the illuminator of one Ignorance only. It has not the power of enlightening much, because its associate is not clear.

This [distributive Ignorance] is the individual's causal body, because it is the cause of the making of 'I,' &c. It is also called 'the sheath of bliss,' because is abounds in bliss and covers like a sheath; and 'dreamless sleep,' because all things repose in it,—on which account it is said to be the scene of the disolution of the subtile and gross body.

Both *Iswara* and *Prajna* experience bliss by means of the very subtile modifications of Ignorance lighted up by Intelligence. As the Veda says, "Prajna, whose sole inlet is the intellect, enjoys bliss" (*Mandukya Upanishad*, 5).

And, as is proved by the experience of one who on rising says, "I slept pleasantly, I was conscious of nothing."

Between these two, the collective and distributive aggregates [of Ignorance], there is no difference; but as there is none between a forest and its trees, or between a lake and its waters.

Nor is there any difference between Iswara and Prajna, who are associated respectively with these [collective and distributive aggregates of Ignorance;] just as there is none between the ether appropriated [*i.e.*, the space occupied] by the forest and that appropriated by the trees composing it,—or between the sky reflected in the lake, and that reflected in its waters.

1 Namely, that small underlying portion of Brahma which forms the individual soul.

2 This word is here made to mean a 'limited intelligence,' such as each individual is. In the sixth verse of the Mandukya Upanishad, however, it is described as "almighty, omniscient, &c.;" and Sankaracharya defines *Prajna* as meaning one who has knowledge of the past and future, and of all objects.

As it is said in the Veda, "This is the lord of all, omniscient, the internal ruler, the source of all, for it is the source and reabsorbent of all creatures"[1] (*Mandukya Upanishad*, 6).

As there is an unappropriated ether, the source of that appropriated by a forest or by its trees, and of that reflected in a lake or its waters—so too, there is Intelligence which is not associated with Ignorance, the source of these two Ignorance-associated Intelligences [Iswara and Prajna]. It is called *the Fourth*. As it is said in the Veda, "They consider that calm, blissful secondless one to be the Fourth. That is Soul,—that is to be known" (*Mandukya*, 7).

This one, the Fourth, pure intelligence, when not discerned as separate from Ignorance, and Intelligence associated with it, like a red-rot iron ball [viewed without discriminating between the iron and the fire], is the literal meaning of the great sentence ['That art Thou']; but when discerned as separate, it is the meaning that is *indicated*.

This Ignorance has two powers, namely, that of (*a*) *envelopment* (or *concealment*), and of (*b*) *projection*.

The power of *envelopment* is such that, just as even a small cloud, by obscuring the beholder's path of vision, seems to overspread the sun's disc, which is many leagues in extent,—so Ignorance, though limited, veiling the understanding of the beholder, seems to cover up Soul, which is unlimited, and unconnected with the universe. As it has been said, "As he whose eye is covered by a cloud, thinks in his delusion that the sun is clouded and has lost its light,—So that Soul which seems bound to him whose mind's eye is blind,—that Soul, essentially eternal perception, and I."[2]

Soul, covered up by this [enveloping power], appears to be an agent and a patient, and to experience pleasure, pain, and other mundane conditions; just as a rope, covered by ignorance as to its real nature, appears to be a snake.

The power of *projection* is such, that, just as ignorance regarding a rope, by its own power raises up the form of a snake, &c., on the rope which is covered by it,—so Ignorance too, by its own power, raises up, on Soul which is covered by it, ether and the whole universe. As it has been said, "The projective power [of Ignorance] can create the world, beginning with subtile bodies, and ending with the terrene orb."[3]

Intelligence, associated with Ignorance possessed of these two powers, is, when itself is chiefly considered, the efficient

1 This is said of *Prajna*. 2 *Hastamalaka*, 12.
3 *Vakyasudha*, v. 13.

cause; and when its associate is chiefly considered, is the material cause. Just as a spider, when itself is chiefly considered, is the efficient cause of its web, the effect,—and when its body is chiefly considered, is the material cause of it.

NOTES ON SECTION IV

In the foregoing pages, two eternal entities have been described, namely, Brahma and Ignorance. These two have been united from everlasting, and the first product of their union is Iswara or God. It should be very distinctly understood that God—"the highest of manifestations in the world of unreality"[1]—is the collective aggregate of all animated things, from the highest deity down to a blade of grass, just as a forest is a collective aggregate of trees.

This, to any ordinary mind, is tantamount to saying that there is no personal God at all; for how can it be supposed that this aggregate of sentiencies has, or has ever had, any power of united action, so as to constitute it a personal Being? Yet, after describing God as identical with the aggregate of individual sentiencies, apart from which he can have no more existence than a forest can have apart from the trees which compose it, the text proceeds to treat him as a personal Being, endowed with the qualities of omniscience, &c., and bearing rule over individual souls!

The attributes assigned to him are thus explained by the commentator. His *'omniscience'* is merely his being a witness of the whole universe, animate and inanimate; or, as the text puts it, He is omniscient as being the illuminator of the whole body of illusion. He is called *'Iswara,'* because he presides over individual souls, and allots rewards according to their works. How this aggregate of individual souls is to preside over itself, and reward each soul included in it according to its works, it is impossible to say;[2] but his functions in this capacity ought to be a sinecure, inasmuch as it is strongly insisted upon that works, whether good or bad, are followed by an exactly proportioned measure of reward or punishment, without the intervention of anybody. He is the *'controller'* in the sense of being the mover or impeller of souls; and the *'internal ruler'* as dwelling in the heart of each, and restraining the intellect. He is the *'cause of the world,'* not as its creator, but as the seat of the evolution of that illusory effect. Indeed, it would be inconsistent to speak of, a creator of a world which has no greater reality than belongs to things seen in a dream!

2. *'Iswara's causal body.'*

As Illusion overlying Brahma is the cause of the production of all things, it is called Iswara's causal or all-originating body. From it originate the super-sensible and sensible elements, then subtile bodies and, lastly, gross bodies. These envelop transmigrating souls like

1 *Calcutta Review*, 1878, p. 314. See also *Rational Refutation*, p. 211.

2 One might as well assert the possibility of a man's sitting on his own shoulders!

sheaths, which have to be successively stripped off to reach pure Brahma.

3. *'Dreamless sleep.'*

There are said to be three states of the soul in respect of the body, viz., waking, dreaming, and dreamless sleep. Brahma is described as 'the fourth' state. "When a man with all his wits about him is wide awake, he is regarded as being furthest removed from the state in which he ought to be,—he being then enveloped in the denset investment of Ignorance. When he sleeps and dreams, he is considered to have shuffled off his outermost coil; therefore a dream is spoken of as the scene of the dissolution of the totality of the gross. The objects viewed in dreams are regarded as 'subtile.' When a man sleeps so soundly that he has no dream, he is regarded as having got rid not only of his 'gross body' but also of his 'subtile body;' hence profound and dreamless sleep is spoken of as the 'scene of the dissolution both of the gross and of the subtile body.' But although, in profound sleep, a man has got rid of all the *developments* of Ignorance, yet he is still wrapped in Ignorance itself, and this must be got rid of. He must not, like the sleeper who 'slept pleasantly and knew nothing,' 'enjoy blessedness by means of the very subtile modifications of Ignorance illuminated by Intellect,' but he must become Intellect simply—identical with Blessedness. To this absolute Unity is given the name of 'the Fourth.' "[1]

The following remarks of Colebrooke's are of interest in this connection:—"In profound sleep the soul is absent, having retired by the channel of the arteries, and being as it were enfolded in the supreme deity. It is not, however, blended with the divine essence, as a drop of water fallen into a lake when it becomes undistinguishable; but, on the contrary, the soul continues discriminate, and returns unchanged to the body which it animates while awake. Swoon or stupor is intermediate between sleep and death. During insensibility produced by accident or disease, there is, as in profound sleep and lethargy, a temporary absence of the soul. In death it has absolutely quitted its gross corporeal frame."[2]

V

FROM Intelligence associated with Ignorance attended by its projective power, in which the quality of insensibility (*tamas*) abounds, proceeds ether,—from ether, air,—from air, heat,—from heat, water,—and from water, earth. As the Veda says, "From this, from this same Self, was the ether produced" (*Taittiriya Upanishad*, 2. 1). The prevalence of insensibility in the cause of these elements is inferred from observing the excess of inanimateness which is in them.[3]

Then, in those elements, ether and the rest, arise the qualities

1 Dr. Ballantyne's *Lecture on the Vedanta*, para. 152(f).

2 Colebrooke's *Essays*, i. 398.

3 "The elements being unenlightened by Intellect, which they quite obscure."—Ballantyne's *Lecture on the Vedanta*.

pleasure, pain, and insensibility, in the proportion in which they exist in their cause. These are what are termed the subtile elements, the rudimentary elements, the non-quintuplicated [lit. 'not become the five,' by combination]

From them spring the subtile bodies and the gross elements

The *'subtile bodies'* are the distinguishing [or evidentiary] bodies, consisting of seventeen members.

The *'members'* are the five organs of sense, mind, and intellect, the five organs of action, and the five vital airs.

the *'organs of sense'* are the ear, skin, eye, tongue, and nose. These arise separately, in order, from the unmingled pleasure-portions of ether and the rest.[1]

'Intellect' is the modification of the internal organ which is characterised by certitude; *'mind'* is the modification characterised by resolution and irresolution; in these two are included thinking and egoism.

'Thinking' is that affection of the internal organ characterised by investigation; *'egoism'* is the affection characterised by self-consciousness. These two arise from the *united* pleasure-endowed portions of ether and the others. That they are the effect of the pleasure-portions of the elements is inferred from their being luminous.

This intellect, together with the organs of sense, forms the cognitional sheath (*vijnanamayakosa*).

This one, which fancies itself to be an agent and a patient, and passes to and fro between this and the other world [*i.e.*, a transmigrating soul], is called the conventional[2] soul.

The mind, together with the organs of action, form the mental [or sensorial] sheath (*manomayakosa*).

The *'organs of action'* are the mouth, hand, foot, anus, and generative organ. These arise, separately, in order, from the unmixed pain-portions of the elements [which are characterised by *activity*].

The *'vital airs'* are respiration (*prana*), inspiration (*apana*), flatuousness (*vyaña*), expiration (*udana*), and digestion (*samana*). *'Respiration'* has an upward motion, and abides in the extremity of the nose; *'inspiration'* has a downward course,

1 That is to say, from ether, the characteristic of which is sound, came the ear,—from air, of which mobility is the characteristic, and in which sound and feel are sensible, came the sense of touch, and so on.

2 "There can be no such thing as a substance existing *conventionally* but not *really*. Things there may be, existing in the opinions of men or implied in their conduct, but if we deny their reality, we can only mean that they are mere fancies, and therefore not actually existing substances. . . . In fact, conventional, as opposed to real, can only mean imaginary, in other words, false."—*Dialogues*, p. 394.

and abides in the anus, &c.; *'flatuousness'* moves in all directions, and pervades the whole body; *'expiration'* belongs to the throat, has an upward course, and is the ascending air; *'digestion'* is the assimilation of solid and liquid food on its reaching the stomach.

'Assimilation' is the causing of digestion, and the production of juice, blood, semen, excrement, &c.

Some persons [followers of Kapila] say that there are five other airs, named Naga, Kurma, Krikara, Devadatta, and Dhananjaya.

'Naga' is that which causes eructation; *'kurma'* is that which causes the opening and closing of the eyes; *'krikara'* causes hunger, and *'devadatta'* yawning; and *'dhananjaya'*[1] is the nourisher.

But others [the Vedantins] say that there are five only, as these are included in the previous five, respiration and the rest.

This set of five vital airs arises from the united pain-portions of the elements, ether and the others. The five, together with the organs of action, form the respiratory sheath. Its being a product of the pain-portions of the elements, is inferred from its being endowed with activity [the characteristic of the *'rajoguna'*].

Of these sheaths, 'the intellectual,' being endowed with the faculty of knowing, is an agent; the 'mental,' having the faculty of desire, is an instrument; and the 'respiratory,' having the faculty of activity, is an effect. This division is in accord with the capabilities of each. These three sheaths together constitute the subtile frame.[2]

Here, too, the totality of the subtile bodies, as the seat of one intellect [*i.e.*, Sutratma's], is a collective aggregate like the forest or the lake; or, as the seat of many intellects [viz., those of individual souls], is a distributive aggregate, like the forest trees or the lake-waters.

Intelligence associated with the collective aggregate [of subtile bodies] is called Sutratma [Thread-soul], Hiranyagarbha, or Prana, because it passes as a thread through all [the subtile frames], and on account of the conceit that it is the five uncompounded elements possessing the faculties of knowing, desire, and activity [*i.e.*, that it is the subtile body itself].

This aggregate, because it is more subtile than the gross organisms, is called His subtile body, consisting of the three

1 This air continues in the body even after death, says the scholiast, quoting from some author: *"na jahati mritanchapi sarvavyapi dhananjayah!"*

2 It attends the soul in its transmigrations.

sheaths, 'the intellectual' and the others; and because it consists of the [continuance of the] waking thoughts, it is called a dream, and is therefore said to be the scene of the dissolution of the gross.[1]

Intelligence associated with the distributive aggregate of subtile organisms is *Taijasa* (the brilliant), because it has the luminous internal organ as its associate.

This distributive aggregate, too, being more subtile than the gross organisms, is called his subtile frame, comprising the three sheaths beginning with 'the intellectual;' and it is said to be a dream because it is made up of the [continuance of the] waking thoughts, on which account it is called the scene of the dissolution of the gross organisms.

These two, the Thread-soul [Sutratma] and Taijasa, by means of the subtile modifications of the mind, have experience of subtile objects. As it is said in the Veda, "Taijasa has fruition of the supersensible" (*Mandukya*, 4).

There is no difference between the collective and distributive aggregates of the subtile frames, or between Sutratma and Taijasa, who are associated with them,—just as there is none between the forest and its trees, or between the space occupied by each,—or between the lake and its waters, and the sky reflected in each.

Thus were the subtile organisms produced.

The gross elements are those that have been made by combining the five [subtile elements]. Quintuplication is on this wise. After dividing each of the five subtile elements, ether and the rest, into two equal parts, and then subdividing each of the first five of the ten moieties into four equal parts, mix those four parts with the others, leaving the [undivided] second moiety of each. As it has been said, "After dividing each into two parts, and the first halves again into four parts, by uniting the latter to the second half of each, each contains the five"[2] (*Panchadasi*, i. 27).

It must not be supposed that there is no authority for this, for from the Vedic passage regarding the combination of three

1 "For, in a dream, the sight of trees and rivers, and the sound of voices, &c., are present to us, without the actual things called trees, &c., being present at all. To the dreamer, the whole external world is as it were not,—and, in the opinion of the Vedantin, to the dreamer it really is not."—*Lecture on the Vedanta*.

2 That is, "the particles of the several elements, being divisible, are, in the first place, split into moieties; whereof one is subdivided into quarters, and the remaining moiety combines with one part (a quarter of a moiety) from each of the four others."—Colebrooke's *Essays*, i. 396. Each of the five elements thus contains a moiety of itself and an eighth of each of the others.

things,[1] the combination of five is implied. Though the five alike contain the five, the name 'ether' and the rest are still applicable[2] to them, in accordance with the saying, "For the sake of distinction, one has this name, and another that" (*Vedanta Sutras*, 2. 4. 22). Then, in ether sound is manifested, —in air, sound and touch,—in heat, sound, touch, and form,—in water, sound, touch, form, and taste,—in earth, sound, touch, form, taste, and smell.

From these quintuplicated elements spring, one above the other, the worlds Bhur, Bhuvar, Swar, Mahar, Janas, Tapas, and Satya; and, one below the other, the nether worlds called Atala, Vitala, Sutala, Rasatala, Talatala, Mahatala, and Patala;[3]—Brahma's egg;—the four kinds of gross bodies included in it; and food and drink.

'The four kinds of gross bodies' are the viviparous, the oviparous, the moisture-engendered, and the germinating.

The viviparous are those produced from the womb, as men and animals; *the oviparous* are those born from eggs, as birds and snakes; *the moisture-engendered* are those which spring from moisture, as lice and gnats; *the germinating* are those which shoot up from the ground, as creepers and trees.

In this case, too, the fourfold gross body, viewed as the seat of one [collective] intellect or of many [individual] intellects, is a collective aggregate like a forest or a lake, or a distributive aggregate like the forest-trees or the lake-waters.

Intelligence associated with the collective aggregate is called Vaiswanara [the spirit of humanity] or Virat;[4] [the former] because of the conceit that it is in the whole of humanity, and [the latter] because it appears in various forms.[5]

This collective aggregate is his gross body. It is called 'the nutrimentitious sheath,' on account of the changes of food [which go on within it and build it up], and it is said to be awake, because it is the scene of the fruition of the gross.

Intelligence associated with the distributive aggregate is called Viswa, because, without abandoning the conceit of the subtile body, it enters into all gross bodies.

The distributive aggregate is his gross body, and is called

1 *Chhandogya Upanishad*, 6. 3. 3.

2 The name 'ether' is suitable to the first because 'ether' largely predominates in it, and so with the other four.

3 For an account of these upper and lower regions, see Wilson's *Vishnu Purana*, ii. 209, 225.

4 Compare *Manu*, i. 32, 33, and *Sanskrit Texts*, v. 369.

5 I have followed the scholast, who says, *Sarvapraninikayeshvaham ityabhimanatwad vaiswanaratwam; nanaprakarena prakasamanatwachcha vairajatwam labhate ityarthah*. Ballantyne's rendering of the last clause is, "Because it rules over the various kinds [of bodies]."

the nutrimentitious sheath on account of the changes of food [which go on within it and build it up]. It is also said to be awake because it is the seat of the fruition of the gross.

Viswa and Vaiswanara have experience of all gross objects; that is, by means of the ear and the rest of the five organs of sense, which are controlled by the quarters, wind, the sun, Varuna, and the Aswins respectively, [they have experience of] sound, sensation, form, taste, and smell;—by means of the mouth and the rest of the five organs of action, which are controlled by Agni, Indra, Upendra, Yama, and Prajapati respectively, [they have experience of] speaking, taking, walking, evacuation, and sensual delights; and by means of the four internal organs, named mind, intellect, egoism, and thinking, which are controlled by the moon, Brahma, Siva, and Vishnu respectively, [they have experience of] doubting, certitude, egoising, and thought. As it is said in the Veda, ["The first quarter is Vaiswanara], who is in the waking state, and has cognition of externals" (*Mandukya Upanishad*, 3).

Here, too, as in the former cases, there is no difference between the distributive and collective aggregates of gross organisms, or between Viswa and Vaiswanara who are associated with them; just as there is none between a forest and its trees, or between a lake and its waters, or between the sky reflected in them.

In this way is the gross produced from the five elements quintuplicated.

NOTES ON SECTION V

1. Recapitulating, then, Brahma is illusory associated with three kinds of bodies:

Firstly, with a casual body, composed of Ignorance or Illusion, which, in the aggregate, is Iswara or God, and, distributively, individual souls or Prajna. It is likened to a state of dreamless sleep.

Secondly, with a subtile body, composed of the five organs of sense and of action, mind, intellect, and the five vital airs, seventeen in all. This, in the aggregate, is called Hiranyagarbha, or the Thread-soul, and, in the distributed state, Taijasa. It is likened to a state of dream.

Thirdly, with a gross body composed of the compounded elements. Viewed in the aggregate, it is called Vaiswanara, and distributively, Viswa. It is likened to the waking state.

A fourth state is that of the unassociated pure Brahma, who is technically styled 'The Fourth.'

2. Mind, intellect, egoism and thinking, which, elsewhere, are styled 'internal organs,' are, collectively, 'the internal organ.' See note elsewhere.

VI

THE aggregate of all these expanses of gross, subtile, and causal bodies is one vast expanse; just as the aggregate of a number of minor [or included] forests is one large forest, or that of a number of minor [or included] bodies of water is one large body.

Intelligence associated with it, from Viswa and Vaiswanara up to Iswara, is one only; just as the space occupied by the various included forests is one, or as the sky reflected in the various included bodies of water is one.

Unassociated Intelligence not seen to be distinct from the great expanse and the Intelligence associated with it, like a heated ball of iron, [in which the iron and the fire are not discriminated,] is the literal [or primary] meaning of the great sentence, "Truly all this is Brahma;" but when seen as distinct, it is what is indicated by that sentence.

Thus 'illusory attribution,' or the superimposing of the unreal upon the Real, has been set forth in general terms. But now, the particular way in which one man imposes this and another that upon the all-pervading [individuated] self is to be declared.

For example, the very illiterate man says that his son is his self; on account of the text of the Veda [*cf. Satapatha Brahmana,* 14. 9. 4. 26], "Self is born as a son;" and because he sees that he has the same love for his son as for himself; and because he finds that if it is well or ill with his son, it is well or ill with himself.

A Charvaka says that the gross body is his self; on account of the text of the Veda [*Taittiriya Upanishad,* 2. 1], "This is man as made up of the extract of food;" and because he sees that a man leaving his own son [to burn], departs himself from a burning house; and because of the experience, "*I* am fat," "*I* am lean."

Another Charvaka says that the organs of sense are his self; on account of the text of the Veda (*Chhandogya Upanishad,* v. 1. 7), "They, the organs of sense (*pranah*), went to Prajapati and said, ['Lord, which of us is the chief?' He said unto them, 'He is chief among you whose departure makes the body seem worthless'];" and because in the absence of the organs of sense the functions of the body cease; and because of the experience, "*I* am blind of one eye." "*I* am deaf."

Another Charvaka says that the vital airs are his self; on account of the text of the Veda (*Taittiriya Upanishad,* 2. 2), "There is another, an inner self, made of the vital airs;" and because in the absence of the vital airs the organs of sense are inactive; and because of the experience, "*I* am hungry," "I am thirsty."

Another Charvaka says that the mind is his self; on account of the text of the Veda (*Taittiriya Upanishad*, 2. 3), "There is another, an inner self, made of the mind;" and because when the mind sleeps the vital airs cease to be; and because of the experience, "*I* resolve," "*I* doubt."

A Bauddha says that intellect is his self; on account of the text of the Veda (*Taittiriya*, 2. 4), "There is another, an inner self, made up of cognition;" and because, in the absence of an agent, an instrument is powerless; and because of the experience, "*I* am an agent," "*I* am a patient."

The Prabhakara and the Tarkika say that ignorance is their self; on account of the text of the Veda (*Taittiriya*, 2. 5), "There is another, an inner self, made up of bliss;" and because, during sleep, intellect and the rest are merged in ignorance; and because of the experience, "*I* am ignorant."

The Bhatta says that Intelligence associated with ignorance is his self; on account of the text of the Veda (*Mandukya Upanishad*, 5), "Self is a mass of knowledge, and comprised of bliss;" and because during sleep there are both the light [of intelligence] and the darkness [of ignorance[1]]; and because of the experience, "Myself I know not."

Another Bauddha says that nihility is his self; on account of the text of the Veda, "In the beginning, this was a mere nonentity;" and because during sleep everything disappears; and because of the experience of the man who has just awoke from sleep,—an experience in the shape of a reflection on his own non-existence,—when he says, "I slept—during sleep, *I* was not."

That these, beginning with 'son' and ending with 'nihility,' have not the nature of self, is now declared. Seeing that, in the fallacies based on Vedic texts, arguments, and personal experience, brought forward by the 'very illiterate man' and the other speakers, each succeeding fallacy refutes the notion of self put forth in that preceding it, it is clear that 'son' and the rest are not the self.

Moreover, from the opposite statements of other strong Vedic texts to the effect that the all-pervading [individuated] self is not gross, not the eye, not the vital airs, not the mind,

1 "For, as the commentator says, referring to the sentence 'I slept pleasantly—I was aware of nothing,' if there were not light or knowledge in the soul, how could the sleeper have known that his sleep was pleasant? And if there were not the absence of light or knowledge, how could he say 'I was aware of nothing'?"—Ballantyne's *Lecture on the Vedanta*.

not an agent, but intelligence, pure intelligence, and existent,—from the transitory character, as of a jar, of the insentient objects beginning with 'son' and ending with 'nihility,' which owe their visibility to Intelligence,—from the force of the experience of the wise, viz., 'I am Brahma,'—and also from the fact that the fallacies based on this and that Vedic passage, argument, and personal experience have been refuted,—each of those from 'son' down to 'nihility' is assuredly not the self.

Therefore, all-pervading [individuated] Intelligence alone, the illuminator of each of those [son and the rest], whose nature is eternal, pure, intelligent, free and true, is the true self—such is the experience of those who know the Vedanta.

NOTES ON SECTION VI

1. The *Charvakas,* otherwise called *Sunyavadins* or *Lokayatikas,* were one of the ancient heretical sects of Hindus. Professor Wilson says of them (*Works,* ii. 87) that they "condemned all ceremonial rites, ridiculed even the Sraddha, and called the authors of the Vedas fools, knaves, and buffoons." He says too that they were "named from one of their teachers, the Muni Charvaka. . . . The appellation Sunyavadi implies the asserter of the unreality and emptiness of the universe; and another designation, Lokayata, expresses their adoption of the tenet, that this being is the *Be-all* of existence; they were, in short, the advocates of materialism and atheism" (*Works,* i. 22). Colebrooke, too, calls their doctrine "undisguised materialism." According to this scholar, their principal tenets were, (*a*) the identity of the soul with the body,—(*b*) the rejection of *akasa* as an element,—and (*c*) the acknowledgment of perception alone as a means of proof. Their doctrines are explained in the first chapter of the *Sarvadarsanasangraha,* which has been translated by Professor Cowell.[1]

2. The *Bauddhas,* or followers of Buddha, are said by Brahmanical controversialists to have been divided into four sects, styled *Madhyamikas, Yogacharas, Sautrantikas,* and *Vaibhashikas.* Those referred to in the text would be the first two, the former of whom are said to have maintained that all is void, and the latter that all is void but intelligence. Possibly these four schools did at one time exist amongst the Indian Buddhists; but it is difficult to understand how they could have held the views ascribed to them in the text. For one of the cardinal doctrines of Buddhism is that *there is no self.* One of the best authorities on Southern Buddhist teaching this wrote:—"The idea of the Brahmans is, that there is a supreme existence, *paramatma,* from which each individual existence has derived its being, but that this separate existence is an illusion; and that the grand object of man is to

[1] *Vide* pamphlet entitled *"The Charvaka System of Philosophy."*—The term *Lokayata, or Lokayatika,* is here explained to be that applied to men who held the opinion, 'widely prevalent in the world' (*lokeshu ayatam vistirnam yanmatam asti*), that wealth and desire are the only ends of man, and that there is no future world.

effect the destruction of the cause of seeming separation, and to secure the reunion of the derived and the underived, the conditioned and the unconditioned. But Buddha repeatedly, by an exhaustive variation of argument, denies that there is any self or ego. Again and again, he runs over the components and essentialities of being, enumerating with tedious minuteness the classifications into which they may be divided, in order to convince his followers that, in whatever way these constituents may be placed, or however they may be arranged, there can be found in them no self."[1] How then could the Buddhists referred to in the text have held 'nihility' or 'intelligence' to be *self?*

3. The *Prabhakaras* were the followers of Prabhakāra, the well-known scholiast of the Purva-Mimansa; the *Tarkikas* are of course the Naiyayikas or followers of the Nyaya. The *Bhattas* are presumably the disciples of Kumarila Bhatta, the well-known Mimansaka already referred to, who lived about a century before Sankaracharya.

VII

THE 'withdrawal' (*apavada*) is the assertion that the whole of the unreal, beginning with Ignorance, which is an illusory effect of the Real, is nothing but the Real; just as a snake, which is the illusory effect of a rope, is nothing whatsoever but the rope.

It has been said, "An actual change of form is called *vikara*, whilst a merely apparent change of form is called *vivartta*." This shall now be illustrated.

The whole of the four classes of gross bodies constituting the seat of enjoyment,—the food and drink necessary for their use,—the fourteen worlds, Bhur and the rest, the repository of these,—and Brahma's egg which is the receptacle of all those worlds,—all these are nothing more than the quintuplicated elements of which they are made.

The quintuplicated elements, with sound and the other objects of sense, and the subtile bodies,—all these are nothing more than the non-quintuplicated elements of which they are made.

The non-quintuplicated elements, with the qualities of goodness and the rest, in the inverse order of their production, are nothing more than Ignorance-associated Intelligence, which is their material cause.

Ignorance,[2] and intelligence associated with it, constituting

1 Hardy's *Legends and Theories of the Buddhists*, p. 171. See also this author's *Manual of Buddhism*, p. 405; and Rhys Davids' *Buddhism*, pp. 90-99.

2 How can *Ignorance* be "nothing more than Brahma," seeing that it is an eternally distinct "entity"?

Iswara, &c., are nothing more than Brahma, the Fourth, the unassociated Intelligence, which forms their substrate.

NOTE ON SECTION VII

The object of the foregoing is to demonstrate that the phenomenal world is nought but the illusory effect (*vivartta*) of the secondless Reality Brahma; who is its illusory material cause. The relation between Brahma and the phenomenal is that of the rope mistaken for a snake, which snake is only an illusion. *Vikara,* on the other hand, which is synonymous with *parinama* (*Amara,* iii. 2. 15), is a real change of form and name. Instances of it are found in the formation of an earring from a lump of gold, or of a jar or toy-elephant from clay, in which there is a change of form and of name, but not of substance; or in the transformation of milk into curds, where there is a change of substance as well as of name and form.

The old Vedantists, as already stated, regarded the phenomenal world as a *vikara* or evolution from Brahma, a view which is strenuously rejected by the moderns[1] or *mayavadins.*

VIII

By means of these two, illusory attribution and its withdrawal, the precise meaning of the words 'That' and 'Thou' [in the sentence 'That art Thou,' '*tat twam asi*'] is determined.

For example, the collective aggregate of Ignorance and the rest, Intelligence associated with it and having the characteristic of omniscience, &c. [*i.e.,* Iswara], and the unassociated Intelligence,—this triad, appearing as one, after the manner of a red-hot iron ball [where the iron and the fire are not viewed as distinct], is the literal [or expressed] meaning of the word 'That;' but, unassaciated Intelligence, the substrate of that which is associated, is its real [or indicated] meaning.

The distributive aggregate of Ignorance and the rest, Intelligence associated with it and having the characteristic of limited knowledge [*i.e.,* Prajna], and Intelligence which is not associated,—this triad, appearing as one, after the manner of a red-hot ball of iron, is the literal meaning of the word 'Thou;' but, pure Intelligence, the Fourth, all-pervading joy, the substrate of that associated Intelligence, is its real meaning.

NOTE ON SECTION VIII

This section prepares the way for the subject to the consideration of which the two succeeding sections are devoted, namely, the identity in meaning of the terms 'That' and 'Thou' in the great Vedantic sentence 'That art Thou.'

"If they cannot be shown to mean the same thing, then the sentence does not enunciate a truth. The author therefore undertakes to show that they do mean the same thing. This he does by showing, as we

1 Their doctrine of existences, already stated, must be borne in mind here.

have just seen, that the only apparent difference between the senses of the two terms is that which appears to exist between Ignorance in its *collective* aggregate and Ignorance in its *distributive* aggregate; and as it has been ruled that these have *no* difference—as there is none between a forest and its trees—it follows that there is no difference in meaning between the term 'That' and the term 'Thou' in the sentence 'That art Thou.' "[1]

IX

Now the great sentence shall be explained.

This sentence, 'That art Thou,' viewed under three different relations, declares what is meant by the Indivisible [or Impartite].

The three relations are—

(a.) The community of reference (*samanadhikaranya*) of the two words ['That' and 'Thou'].

(b.) The position of predicate and subject (*viseshana-viseshyabhava*) occupied by the things referred to by the words,—and

(c.) The connection as indicated and indicator (*lakshya-lakshanabhava*), between the purport of the two words and individuated self.

As it has been said, "Between the things which the words refer to, and individuated self (*pratyagatman*), there is community of reference, the connection as predicate and subject, and as indicated and indicator."[2]

(a.) *Community of reference.*

As. in the sentence 'that is this same Devadatta,'[3] the words 'that' and 'this,' which respectively distinguish the Devadatta of a former and of the present time, are connected by the fact that they both refer to one and the same Devadatta;—so, in the sentence 'That art Thou,' the words 'That' and 'Thou,' which indicate Intelligence characterised respectively by invisibility and visibility, have the connection of reference to one and the same Intelligence.

(b.) *Connection as predicate and subject.*

As, in that same sentence ['That is this same D.'], the relation of predicate and subject exists between the Devadatta of the former time, who is referred to in the word 'That,' and the Devadatta of the present time, referred to in the word 'this,'—a relation constituted by the exclusion of the difference [of time] which there is between them,—so, too, in this sentence

1 *Lecture on the Vedanta.*

2 *Naishkarmyasiddhi,* iii. 3.

3 *I.e.,* 'That person whom I saw on some former occasion in this same Devadatta whom I now behold.'—Ballantyne's *Lecture on the Vedanta.*

['That art Thou'] is there the relation of predicate and subject between Intelligence distinguished by invisibility, as indicated by the word 'That,' and Intelligence distinguished by visibility, as indicated by the word 'Thou,'—a relation constituted by the exclusion of the difference which there is between them.

(c.) *Connection as indicator and indicated.*

As in that sentence ['That is this D.'], by the omission of the contradictory characteristics of former and present time, the words 'that' and 'this,' or the things they refer to, hold the relation of indicator and indicated with respect to the non-contradictory [or common] term 'Devadatta;'— so, too, in this sentence ['That art Thou'], by the omission of the conflicting characteristics of invisibility and visibility, the words 'That' and 'Thou,' or the things represented by them, hold the relation of indicator and indicated with respect to the non-conflicting [or common] term 'Intelligence.'

This is what is called [in Alankara] 'the indication of a portion'[1] (*bhagalakshana*).

NOTE ON SECTION IX

Bhagalakshana.

According to Hindu rhetoricians, the meaning of every word or sentence comes under one of three heads, that is, it is either literal (*vachya*), indicative (*lakshya*), or suggestive (*vyangya*). Their three functions or power are termed Denotation (*abhidha*), Indication (*lakshana*), and Suggestion (*vyanjana*). We are here concerned with the middle one only, which is thus defined in the *Kavyaprakasa* (ii. 9): "When the literal meaning is incompatible [with the rest of the sentence], and, either from usage or from some motive, another meaning is indicated, in connection with the primary one, that imposed function is called 'Indication.' "

The sentence "A herd-station on the Ganges" is an example of this. Here the *literal* meaning of the word 'Ganges' is *incompatible* with the rest of the sentence, it being impossible that the herdsmen could be living on the surface of the water; so it is clear that the river's 'bank' is *indicated,* and this meaning is *imposed* upon the word 'Ganges' in accordance with *usage.* In using the word 'Ganges' rather than 'bank of the Ganges,' there is also the *motive* of conveying the idea of coolness, purity, &c., which might not be equally well suggested by the use of the latter expression.

There are numerous varieties of 'Indication'—according to the author of the *Sahityadarpana,* there are as many as eighty—but the two principal ones, and those which alone concern us, are—

(1.) Inclusive Indication (*upadana-ldkshana*), and

(2.) Indicative Indication (*lakshana-lakshana*).

The former is described in the *Kavyaprakasa* (ii. 10) as that which

1 Cf. *Adhyatma Ramayana-Uttarakanda,* v. 27.

introduces something else in order to establish itself, and the latter as that which abandons itself in order to introduce something else.

An example of 'Inclusive Indication' is "The white is galloping," the literal sense of which is impossible, whilst what is indicated is "The white *horse* is galloping." Thus the word 'horse' is introduced without the abandonment of the term 'white.' This class is therefore sometimes called *'ajahatswartha'* or *'ajahallakshana,'* Indication in which there is the use of a word *without* the abandonment of its sense.

An example of 'Indicative Indication,' or Indication simply, is the sentence already given, "A herd-station on the Ganges," where the word 'Ganges' abandons its own meaning in order to introduce that of the 'bank.' This class is therefore sometimes called *'jahatswartha,'* or *'jahallakshana,'* Indication in which there is the use of a word *with* the abandonment of its meaning.

Now the *bhagalakshana* of the text is a combination of these two varieties, and is therefore otherwise called *jahadajahallakshana.* This term is defined in the *Vachaspatya* as "Indication abiding in one part of the expressed meaning, whilst another part of it is abandoned. As, for example, in the sentence 'That is this Devadatta,' whilst the meanings expressive of past and present time are abandoned, another portion of the expressed meaning remains and conveys the idea of the one Devadatta. And again, in the sentence 'That art thou, Swetaketu,' whilst there is the abandonment of the conflicting ideas of omniscience and parviscience, there is, as in the other example, the retention of one portion which conveys the idea of Intelligence only."[1]

These two varieties of Indication must be thoroughly understood in order to comprehend the purport of the following Section.

X

IN the sentence 'That art Thou,' the *literal* meaning is not suitable as it is in such a sentence as 'The lotus is blue.' For, in the latter, the literal sense suits because there is no valid reason for not accepting the fact that the quality denoted by the term 'blue,' and the substance denoted by the term 'lotus,' —inasmuch as they exclude such other qualities and substances as 'white' and 'cloth'—are mutually connected as subject and predicate, or are identical, each being qualified by the other.[2]

But, in the former sentence, the literal meaning does not suit, because there is the evidence of our senses against the acceptance of a connection as subject and predicate, between Intelligence distinguished by invisibility as denoted by the term 'That,' and Intelligence distinguished by visibility as denoted by the term 'Thou,'—a connection constituted by the

1 *Vide Vachaspataya,* s.v. *Jahadajahallakshana.*

2 The 'lotus' being the thing that we call 'blue', and the 'blue' thing being what we call 'lotus.'—*Ballantyne.*

exclusion of their mutual differences:—and also against our regarding them as identical, each being qualified by the other.

Nor, again, is it consistent to regard it as an example of 'Indication in which the primary sense is abandoned'[1] (*jahallakshana*), as is the case in the sentence 'The herdsman lives on the Ganges.' For, as the literal sense, which places the Ganges and the herdsman in the relation of location and thing located, is altogether incongruous, whilst an appropriate sense is obtained by abandoning the literal meaning altogether and regarding it as indicating the 'bank' connected with it,—it is rightly regarded as an example of 'Indication in which the primary sense is abandoned.'

But, in the other case, as the literal sense, which expresses the identity of the Intelligences characterised severally by invisibility and visibility, is only partially incongruous,—and so, unless we abandon the remaining part, it would be inappropriate to consider something else to be indicated,—it is not proper to regard it as an instance of 'Indication in which the primary sense is abandoned.'

And it must not be said, "As the word 'Ganges' abandons its own meaning and indicates the 'bank,' so let the word 'That' or 'Thou' abandon its own meaning and indicate the word 'Thou' or 'That,' and then *jahallakshana* would not be incongruous." For, in the one case, as there is no distinct notion of the word 'bank,' because it is not heard, there is need for the conveyance of that notion by Indication; but as the words 'That' and 'Thou' *are* heard, and there is a distinct perception of their sense, there is no need of the reconveyance of the perception of the sense of each by the other, by means of Indication.

Further, it cannot be regarded as an instance of '*ajahallakshana*,' as is the case in the sentence "The red is running."[2] For, as the literal sense, which denotes the motion of the quality 'red,' is incongruous, whilst it is possible to avoid that incongruity by perceiving that a 'horse,' or other animal, is indicated as the seat of the redness, without the abandonment of the term 'red,'—it is right to regard it as an instance of 'Indication in which the primary sense is not abandoned' (*ajahallakshana*).

But, in the other case, as the literal sense, namely, the identity of the Intelligence distinguished severally by invisibility and visibility, is incongruous, and the incongruity is not

1 *Vide* Note on preceding Section.
2 *Vide* Note on preceding Section.

removed by regarding something else connected therewith as indicated without the abandonment of the contradictory terms, the sentence does not stand as an example of that kind of Indication.

And it must not be said, "Let the word 'That' or 'Thou' abandon the incongruous portion of its meaning,[1] and, retaining the other portion,[2] indicate the meaning of the word 'Thou' or 'That'[3] respectively; then there will be no need of explaining it in another way as '*bhagalakshana*' or the 'Indication of a portion.' " For it is impossible for one word to indicate a portion of its own meaning and the meaning of another word; and, further, there is no expectation of the perception of the meaning of either word again by means of Indication, when its meaning has been already perceived by the use of a separate word.

Therefore, as, on account of the incongruity of a portion of its literal meaning which denotes a Devadatta who is distinguished by both past and present time, the sentence 'That is this Devadatta,' or its purport, by abandoning the portion characterised by the contradictory terms past and present time, indicates merely the non-contradictory portion, namely, Devadatta himself,—so, in like manner, on account of the incongruity of a portion of its literal sense which denotes the identity of Intelligences characterised by invisibility and visibility, the sentence 'That art Thou,' or its purport, abandons the portion characterised by the conflicting terms invisibility and visibility, and indicates merely the non-conflicting portion, namely, the Indivisible Intelligence.

NOTE ON SECTION X

"This view of the matter may be illustrated algebraically. Not being able to admit as an equation the expression 'Devadatta + past time + Devadatta + present time,' we reflect that the conception of *time* is not essential to the conception of D's nature; and we strike it out of both sides of the expression, which then gives 'Devadatta = Devadatta,' the equality being that of identity. In the same way, not being able to admit as an equation the expression 'Soul = invisibility = Soul + visibility,' we reflect that the visibility &c., are but the modifications of Ignorance, which, we were told, is no 'reality.' Deleting the unessential portion of each side of the expression, we find 'Soul = Soul,' the equality being here also that of identity."[4]

It must be understood that this Section is closely connected with

1 Viz., that of invisibility or visibility, respectively.

2 Viz., that of Intelligence.

3 *I.e.,* Intelligence characterised by parviscience, &c., or by omniscience, c., respectively.

4 *Lecture on the Vedanta.*

the Ninth, and must be read with it. The two are here disconnected in order to introduce the explanation of a technicality.

XI

THE meaning of the sentence "I am Brahma," [the expression of] the experience [of the instructed pupil] shall now be explained.

When, after making clear the meaning of the words 'That' and 'Thou' by means of the erroneous attribution and its subsequent withdrawal, the teacher has communicated the meaning of the Indivisible by means of the sentence ['That art Thou'], then a modification of the internal organ (*chittavritti*) assuming the form of the Indivisible, arises within the qualified person, and he says. "I am Brahma, the unchanging, pure, intelligent, free, undecaying, supreme joy, eternal, secondless."

That modification of the internal organ, being accompanied by the reflection of Intelligence, and being directed towards the previously unrecognised Supreme Brahma, non-different from individuated self, drives away the ignorance which invests him. Then, as, when the threads composing a piece of cloth are burned, the cloth itself is consumed, so, when Ignorance, the cause of all effects, is destroyed, every effect ceases; and therefore the modification of the internal organ which has assumed the form of the Indivisible, being one of those effects, also ceases.

As the light of a lamp, unable to illuminate the sun's light, is overpowered by it, so, too, the Intelligence which is there reflected in that modification of the internal organ being incapable of illuminating the Supreme Brahma, non-different from individuated self, is overpowered by it; and its associate, the modification of the internal organ [shaped] on the Indivisible, having been destroyed, it becomes [*i.e.*, merges into] the Supreme Brahma, non-different from individuated self; just as, on the removal of a mirror, the face reflected in it lapses into the face itself.

Such being the case, the two Vedic sayings, "He [Brahma] is to be perceived by the mind alone,"[1] and "He [Brahma] whom with the mind one thinks not,"[2] are not contradictory. For whilst the need of the pervasion by the modification of the internal organ is admitted, [for the cognition of the veiled Brahma, as of other unknown objects], the need of its pervading the result [viz., the unveiled Brahma] is denied. As it has been said,[3] "For the removal of the ignorance [resting] on

1 *Brihadaranyaka*, vi. 4. 19.
2 *Kenopanishad*, i. 5.
3 ?

Brahma, its pervasion by the modification of the internal organ is requisite; but the authors of the Sastras deny that [in His case] there is need of its pervading the result." For, "As Brahma is self-luminous, the light [necessary for illuminating the jar, &c.] is not employed [in His case]."[1]

When the modification of the internal organ assumes the shape of an *inanimate* object, the case is different. For example, [in the cognition] 'This is a jar,' the modification of the internal organ which assumes the shape of the jar is directed towards the unknown object, jar, removes the ignorance which rests on it, and, at the same time, illuminates it, though insentient, with the light of its own indwelling Intelligence. As it has been said,[2] "The internal organ and the light of Intelligence abiding in it, both pervade the jar; then, the ignorance [covering the jar] disappears by means of the former, whilst the jar bursts forth by means of the latter." Just as the light of a lamp directed towards a jar or other object standing in the dark dispels the darkness enveloping it, and by its own brilliance brings it to view.[3]

NOTE ON SECTION XI

From this passage we learn that when the meaning of the great sentence 'That art Thou' has been explained to the pupil and understood by him, he perceives the Indivisible and realises his oneness with Him.

According to the Vedanta, perception of an object, such as a jar, takes place in the following way. When the eye is fixed upon the jar, the internal organ, with the Intelligence appropriated to or reflected in it, goes out towards it, and by its light dispels the darkness of Ignorance enveloping it, illuminates it, *assumes its shape,* and so cognises it. The stock illustration of this is that of water flowing from a well or tank by means of a narrow open channel, emptying itself into the square beds with raised edges, into which a field is sometimes divided for the purpose of irrigation, and assuming the shape

1 ? 2 ?

3 In the passage in the preceding page, I have taken the word *vyapyatwa* in a non-technical sense on the authority of the commentary *Subodhini,* which reads thus:—"*Antahkaranavrittir avarananivrittyartham ajnanavachchhinnachaitanyam vyapnotityetadvrittivyapyatwam angikriyate | Avaranabhanganantaram swayam prakasamanam chaitanyam phalachaitanyam, ityuchyate, asmin phalachaitanye nishkalanke chittavrittir na vyapnoti, avaranabhangasya prageva jatatwena prayojanabhavad ityarthah |* " The modification of the internal organ pervades the ignorance-appropriated Intelligence, in order to remove the covering, and the need of that pervasion is admitted. The Intelligence that shines forth of itself after the destruction of the covering is called '*phalachaitanya;*' the modification of the internal organ does not pervade that spotless *phalachaitanya,* for, since it existed before the destruction of the covering, such pervasion is unnecessary."

of those beds. The illuminated internal organ is the water, and the operation is called an evolution or 'modification' of that organ. As pointed out in the text, however, the perception of Brahma differs from that of an ordinary object, in that He, being self-luminous, is not revealed by the light of the Intelligence reflected in the internal organ, but shines forth as soon as the latter has dispelled the Ignorance enveloping Him.

The word which I have here rendered 'internal organ' is more properly 'thought,' which is a component part of that organ.

XII

As, up to the time of the immediate cognition of Intelligence, which is his own essence, it is necessary to practise (a.) hearing (*sravana*), (b.) consideration (*manana*), (c.) profound contemplation (*nididhyasana*), and (d.) meditation (*samadhi*), these are now set forth.

(a.) 'Hearing' is the ascertaining of the drift of all the Vedantic writings regarding the secondless Reality, by the use of the sixfold means of knowledge[1] (*linga*). These means are (1) the beginning and the ending, (2) repetition, (3) novelty, (4) the result, (5) persuasion, and (6) illustration from analogy. As it has been said.[2] "The beginning and the ending, repetition, novelty, the result, persuasion, and illustration from analogy, are the means for the determination of the purport."

1. 'The beginning and the ending' (*upakramopasamharau*) are the mention at the beginning and end of a chapter of the subject to be expounded in it; as in the 6th chapter of the Chhandogya Upanishad, at the beginning of which, the secondless Reality who is to be set forth in it, is declared in the words "One only without a second," and at the end, in the words "All this is the essence of That."

2. 'Repetition' (*abhyasa*) is the repealed declaration in a chapter of the subject which is to be set forth in it; as, for example, in that same chapter, the secondless Reality is set forth nine times in the words "That art Thou."

3. 'Novelty' (*apurvata*) is the fact that the subject to be treated of in a chapter is not an object of perception by any other means; as, for example, in that same chapter, the secondless Reality [there set forth] is not an object of perception by any other means.

4. 'The result (*phala*) is the motive, set forth in various places, for acquiring the knowledge of Self who is to be treated of in a chapter, or for carrying that knowledge into practice; as, for example, in that same chapter (vi. 14, 2), where it says, "The man who has a teacher knows [the truth], but he is

1 *Lingam artham gamayati.* Sch. 2 ?

delayed [from absorption] until he is set free [by death]; then he attains to it,"—the acquisition of the secondless Reality is forth as the motive for acquiring the knowledge of Him.

5. 'Persuasion'[1] (*arthavada*) is the praising, in various places, the subject to be treated of in a chapter; just as, in that same chapter (vi. 1, 3), the secondless Reality is praised in these words,—"Didst thou ask for that instruction by which the unheard of becomes heard;—the unthought, thought,—the unknown, known?"

6. "Illustration from analogy' (*upapatti*) is an argument stated in various places in support of the subject to be treated of in a chapter; as, for example, in that same chapter (vi. 1, 4), in demonstrating the secondless Reality, an agrument is set forth as follows, to show that the variety of forms [in the universe] rests upon a foundation of words[2] and nothing else,—"O, gentle one! as, by means of one lump of earth, everything earthen is known to be a thing resting upon words alone, a change of form, a name, and nothing in reality but earth, [so is it with the phenomenal world which is nought but Brahma]."

(b.) 'Consideration' is unceasing reflection on the secondless Reality which has been heard of, in conjunction with arguments in support of the Vedanta.

(c.) 'Profound contemplation' is the continuance of ideas consistent with the secondless Reality, to the exclusion of the notion of body and suchlike things which are inconsistent [with Him].

(d.) 'Meditation' is of two kinds, viz:

1. *With* recognition of subject and object (*savikalpaka*), and
2. *Without* such recognition (*nirvikalpaka*).

(1.) 'Meditation with the recognition of subject and object' is the resting of the modification of the internal organ on the secondless Reality whose shape it has assumed, *without* any concern as to the merging of the distinction between the knower and the knowledge, &c. Then, just as there is the perception of earth [and of that alone], even though there be the appearance of an earthen toy-elephant, &c., so too is there the perception of the secondless Reality [alone], even though there be the appearance of duality. As it has been said by those

1 "'Persuasion' is the setting forth of the end, *i.e.*, of the motive; that is to say, it is a speech intended to commend the object of an injunction. For a persuasive speech, by means of laudation, &c., commends the object of an injunction with a view to our quickly engaging [in the performance of the ceremony enjoined]."—Ballantyne's *Aphorisms of the Nyaya*, ii. 63 (b).

2 *Vacharambhana* = *vagalambana*. (*Bhashya* on the *Upanishad*).

engaged [in such contemplation]:—"I am that secondless one who is ever free, whose essence is knowledge, like the ether [*i.e.*, pure and formless], supreme, once seen [that is, never changing, as the moon, &c., does], unborn, alone, everlasting, undefiled [by contact with Ignorance, &c.], all-pervading; I am pure knowledge, whose essence is unvariableness; I am neither fettered nor set free" (*Upadesasahasri*, verses 73 and 74).

(2.) 'Meditation without the recognition of subject and object' is the resting of the modification of the understanding on the secondless Reality whose shape it has assumed, *with* concern as to the merging of the distinction of knower and knowledge, &c., so as to be completely identified with Him. Then, just as, owing to the disappearance of salt after it has [melted and so] assumed the shape of the water [into which it was thrown], nothing appears but the water,[1] so, by the disappearance of the modification of the internal organ after it has assumed the shape of the secondless Reality, nothing appears but the latter.

It must not be supposed that this state and sound sleep are identical; for, though in both alike the modification of the internal organ is not perceived, there is nevertheless this one distinction between them, that it is present in the former [though unperceived], but not in the latter.[2]

NOTES ON SECTION XII

1. *'Profound contemplation is,'* &c.

I am doubtful of the rendering. The text of the Calcutta edition of 1875 stands thus:—*Vijatiyadehadipratyayarahitadwitiyavastusajatiyapratyayapravahah nididhyasanam.* That used by Ballantyne, and adopted too in the St. Petersburg edition of 1877, reads as follows:—*Vijatiyadehadipratyayarahitadvitiyavastuni tadakarakaritaya buddheh sajatiyapravaho nididhyasanam.* It is thus translated by Ballantyne: "'Contemplation' is the homogeneous flow of the understanding mirroring its object, when this object is the Real, &c., to the exclusion of the notion of body or any other thing heterogeneous [to the one Reality mirrored in the understanding]."

2. *'I am the secondless one,'* &c.

This passage is a quotation from Sankaracharya's *Upadesasahasri*, but it is also found in the closing portion of the *Muktikopanishad*. The opening verses of this Upânishad, which is said to belong to the White Yajur Veda (!), introduce us to a scene 'in the charming city of Ayodhya,' where Rama, attended by Sita, his brothers, and various sages, is addressed by Maruti, as the Supreme Self, the embodiment of existence, intelligence, and joy, and is asked to make known to him the way of escape from the fetters of transmigration. The

1 Compare *Chhandogya Upanishad*, vi. 13.

2 *Rational Refutation*, p. 224, but cf. *Yoga Aphorisms*, i. 10.

sectarianism and style of this Upanishad stamp it as modern;[1] and it doubtless copied from the *Upadesasahasri,* not only the passage quoted in our text, but other verses in immediate connection with it.

The author of the Vedantasara does not cite the passage as a quotation from the Veda, as he invariably does when quoting from an Upanishad, but ushers it in with the words *'taduktam abhiyuktaih.'*

The passage as given in the Vedantasara differs in some respects from the original, as will be seen by comparing the two.

Upadesasahasri

Drisisvarupam gaganopamam param
Sakridvibhatam tvajamekam aksharam |
Alepakam sarvagatam yadadwyam
Tadeva chaham satatam vimukta Om || 73

Drisistu suddho 'hamavikriyatmako
Na me 'sti kaschidvishayah svabhavatah |
[*Purastiraschordhvamadhascha sarvatah*
Sampurnabhuma tvaja atmani sthitah] ||74.

Vedantasara (Calc. 1875)

Drisisvarupam gaganopamam param
Sakridvibhatam tvajam ekam avyayam |
Alepakam sarvagatam yadadwyam
Tadeva chaham satatam vimuktam ||
Drisistu suddho 'ham avikriyatmako
Na me 'sti bandho na cha me vimokshah |.

The actual reading in the last line is *baddho,* which is clearly a misprint.

3. For various explanations of the technical terms *savikalpaka* and *nirvikalpaka,*[2] see Ballantyne's *Tarkasangraha* (2nd edition), para 46; Translation of *Sahitya Darpana,* p. 52 (note); and Cowell's Translation of *Kusumanjali,* p. 20 (note).

XIII

THE means [to *nirvikalpaka* meditation] are—

1. Forbearance (*yama*).
2. Minor religious observances (*niyama*).
3. Religious postures (*asana*).
4. Regulation of the breath (*pranayama*).
5. Restraint of the organs of sense (*pratyahara*).
6. Fixed attention (*dharana*).
7. Contemplation (*dhyana*).
8. Meditation (*samadhi*).

1. Acts of 'forbearance' are, sparing life, truthfulness, not stealing, chastity, and non-acceptance of gifts (*aparigraha*).[3]

1 See Weber's *History of Indian Literature,* p. 165.

2 With these two kinds of meditation compare the *'samprajnata'* and *'asamprajnata'* of the Yoga philosophy. The former is 'meditation with an object,' and the latter 'meditation without an object.'

3 *Bhogasadhananam anangikarah.* Bhojaraja on *Yoga,* ii. 30.

2. 'Minor religious observances' are, purification, contentment, endurance of hardships, inaudible repetition of sacred texts (*svadhyaya*), and concentration of the thoughts on Iswara.

3. The 'religious postures' are distinguished by particular positions of the hands and feet, such as *Padmasana*, *Svastikasana*, and others.

4. 'Religion of the breath' consists of the methods of restraining it known as *rechaka*, *puraka*, and *kumbhaka*.

5. 'Restraint of the organs of sense' is the holding them back from their several objects of sense.

6. 'Fixed attention' is the fixing of the internal organ upon the secondless Reality.

7. 'Contemplation' is the continuing of the modification of the internal organ upon the secondless Reality, at intervals.

8. 'Meditation' is that already described as accompanied by the recognition of subject and object (*savikalpaka*).

To the meditation without recognition of subject and object, to which the above are subservient, there are four obstacles, viz.—

1. Mental inactivity (*laya*).
2. Distraction (*vikshepa*).
3. Passion (*kashaya*), and
4. The tasting of enjoyment (*rasaswada*).

1. 'Mental inactivity' is the drowsiness of the medification of the internal organ while not resting on the secondless Reality.

2. 'Distraction' is the resting of the modification of the internal organ on something else, instead of its abiding on the secondless Reality.

3. 'Passion' is the not resting on the secondless Reality, by reason of the impeding of the modification of the internal organ by lust or other desire, even though there be no mental inactivity or distraction.

4. The 'tasting of enjoyment' is the experience of pleasure on the part of the modification of the internal organ, in the recognition of subject and object, while it is not resting on the secondless Reality; or it is the experiencing of such pleasure when about to commence meditation without the recognition of subject and object.

When the internal organ, free from these four hindrances, and motionless as a lamp, sheltered from the wind, exists as the indivisible Intelligence only, then is realised that which is called meditation without recognition of subject and object.

It has been said,[1] "When the internal organ has fallen into a state of inactivity, one should arouse it,—when it is distracted, one should render it quiescent [by turning away from objects of sense, &c.],—when it is affected by passion, one should realise the fact,—when quiescent, one should not disturb it. One should experience no pleasure [during discriminative meditation], but become free from attachment by means of discriminative intelligence." And again[2]—"As [the flame of] a lamp standing in a sheltered spot flickers not," &c.

NOTES ON SECTION XIII

The eight means of promoting *nirvikalpaka* meditation, which are enumerated in the text, are taken from the Yoga Aphorisms, ii. 29; and the definitions of the eight are from the same source, namely, ii. 30-53, and iii. 1-3. The first two, *yama* and *niyama,* are also described in Manu iv. 204 (Sch.).

'Religious postures.'

Padmasana is thus described by Monier Williams in his Sanskrit Lexicon:—"A particular posture in religious meditation, sitting with the thighs crossed, with one hand resting on the left thigh, the other held up with the thumb upon the heart, and the eyes directed to the tip of the nose." The *Rudrayamala,* however, defines it as simply sitting with the left foot on the right thigh and the right foot on the left thigh. To this, the *Tantrasara* adds the following direction:—*"Angushthau cha nibadhniyaddhastabhyam vyutkramat tatah"*—which may possibly mean, "And he should retain the big toes [in their position] by means of the hands in the reverse order," *i.e.,* the left hand on the right foot and the right hand on the left foot (?).

Svastikasana is described by *Vachaspatimisra* as sitting with the left foot doubled up under the right knee and the right foot under the left knee, and the *Tantrasara* adds that the body must be erect. (Vide *Vachaspatya* s. v. *asana.*)

'Regulation of the breath' (*pranayama*).

"The first act is expiration, which is performed through the right nostril, whilst the left is closed with the fingers of the right hand: this is called *Rechaka.* The thumb is then placed upon the right nostril and the fingers raised from the left, through which breath is inhaled: this is called *Paraka.* In the third act, both nostrils are closed and breathing suspended: this is *Kumbhaka.* And a succession of these operations is the practice of *Pranayama."*—(Wilson's *Vishnu Purana,* v. 231.)

1 *Gaudapada's Karikas,* iii. 44, 45.

2 *Bhagavadgita,* vi. 19. The whole verse is—"As [the flame of] a lamp standing in a sheltered spot flickers not, this is regarded as an illustration of a mind-restrained Yogi who is practising concentration of mind."

XIV

THE characteristics of the 'liberated but still living' (*jivanmukta*) are now to be described.

The 'liberated but still living' is he who by knowing the indivisible, pure Brahma, who is his own essence, [a result brought about] by the removal of the Ignorance enveloping Him, perceives Him clearly as the Indivisible and his own essence; and, in consequence of the removal of Ignorance and its effects, such as accumulated works, doubt, and error, remains intent on Brahma,[1] freed from all fetters. As it is said in the Sruti,[2] "When he who is supreme and not supreme (*paravara*) is seen, the fetter of the heart is burst, all doubts are removed, and works[3] fade away."

On arising from meditation, though he sees that, by his body, which is the receptacle of flesh, blood, urine, filth, &c., —by his organs, which are the seat of blindness, slowness, unskilfulness, &c.,—and by his internal organ, which is the seat of hunger, thirst, sorrow, infatuation, &c.,—works are being done according to the previous bent of each; and that he is experiencing the fruit of those which have already commenced to take effect, and yet his knowledge is not interfered with,—he regards them not as real because they have been cancelled. Just as one watching what he knows to be a conjuring performance does not regard it as a reality. It is said, too, in the Sruti,[4] "Though he has eyes, he is as though he had them not; though he has ears, he is as though he had none; though he has a mind, he is as one without a mind; though he has vital airs, he is as though he had them not." And again it has been said,[5] "He who, when awake, is as though in a sound sleep, and sees not duality, or, if seeing it, regards it as non-duality,—who, though acting, is free from [the results of] actions, he, and he alone, is, without doubt, the knower of Self." Just as he continues the practices of eating, walking about, &c., which existed before the attainment of true knowledge, so too he either follows good desires alone, or is indifferent to both good and bad alike. It has been said,[6] "If he who knows the secondless Reality may act as he likes, what difference is there between the knowers of truth

1 Dr. Hall renders '*brahmanishthah*' by 'abides in Brahma,' but the commentator explains it by '*Brahmani nishtha tadekaparata yasga.*'

2 *Mundakopanishad*, 2. 2. 8.

3 Those of the present or of a former birth which have not begun to bear fruit; but *not* those which brought about his present existence.—*Bhashya.*

4 ?

5 *Upadesasahasri*, verse 85.

6 *Naishkarmyasiddhi*, iv. 60.

and dogs in respect of eating impure food? Except the fact of knowing Brahma, there is no difference; the one knows the Self, and the other [the dog] does not."

In that state, humility, &c., which are means of acquiring right apprehension, and good qualities, such as friendliness, &c., cling to him merely as ornaments. It has been said,[1] "Qualities such as friendliness, and the like, exist without an effort in one who has attained to the knowledge of Self, but are not of the nature of means [to that end]." To conclude:—Experiencing, for the sustentation of his body only, the fruits of works which have begun to take effect, which are characterised by pleasure or pain, and are brought about by his own desire, or without any desire on his part, or at the desire of another,—and illuminating the reflections on his internal organ,—when the fruits of his works are exhausted, and his vital airs merge in the supreme Brahma who is all-pervading happiness, then, owing to the destruction of Ignorance and also of the germs of its effects, he abides the Indivisible Brahma who is absolute isolation, whose sole essence is joy, and who is free from all appearance of change. As the Sruti says,[2] "His vital airs ascend not" [*i.e.*, do not transmigrate], but are dissolved within him; and[3]—"He already free [though in the body], is freed [from future embodiments]."

NOTES ON SECTION XIV

1. '*Jivanmukta.*'

This position of the 'liberated but still living' man closely resembles that of the Buddhist *Arhat* or *Rahat.* At death, the latter enters *Nirwana,* that is, ceases to exist,[4]—whilst the former, absorbed into Brahma, enters upon an unconscious and stone-like existence!

2. '*Works.*'

According to the Systems, works are of three kinds, viz., accumulated (*sanchita*), fructescent (*prarabdha*), and current (*kriyamana*). The first are the works of former births which have not yet borne fruit; the second are those which have resulted in the present life, and so have begun to bear fruit; and the third are those which are being performed during the present life, and which will bear fruit in a future one. According to the Vedanta, the true knowledge of Brahma and of one's own identity with Him burns up the accumulated works and cancels the effects of the current ones. The fruits of the fructescent ones must be exhausted during the present life, and then at death emancipation is realised. These last

1 *Naishkaranyasiddhi,* iv. 67.
2 *Brihadaranyaka,* 5. 4. 6 (p. 856).
3 *Kathopanishad,* v. 1 (p. 133).
4 Spence Hardy's *Manual of Buddhism,* p. 40, and *Eastern Monachism,* p. 290.

cannot be destroyed by the knowledge of Brahma; but, according to the Yoga, the meditation which is styled in that system *asamprajnata*, 'meditation without an object,'[1] *can* destroy them, and so is considered by Yogins to be superior to knowledge.[2]

It will interest the Marathi student to notice that the common word *prarabdha*, 'fate,' 'destiny,' is just this technical term explained above—works which have begun to take effect, and the fruit of which it is impossible to evade.

3. *'Supreme and not supreme.'*

'Supreme' as cause, 'not supreme' as effect, says the scholiast. It might also be rendered, 'The First and the Last,' that is, the all-inclusive entity. The fetter of the heart consists of desires resulting from Ignorance.

4. *'If he who knows the secondless Reality,'* &c.

This passage, in the original, consists of a verse and a half, and reads as follows:—

> *Buddhadvaitasatattvasya yatheshtacharanam yadi* |
> *Sunam tattvadrisanchaiva ko bhedo 'suchibhakshane* ||
> *Brahmavittvantatha muktva sa atmajno na chetarah* |

Now the first couplet is also quoted in the *Panchadasi*, iv. 55, and is ascribed by the scholiast to *Suresvara*, the reputed disciple of Sankaracharya; and laboriously following that clue, I at length found the passage in his *Naishkarmyasiddhi*. It is introduced into the *Panchadasi* in support of an appeal to the enlightened man to avoid evil lest he lose the benefits of his knowledge; and its aim is to show that if one who knows the truth throws off all restraints and acts as he likes, he is no better than a dog. That Suresvara, too, disapproved of *yatheshtacharana* is evident from the context of the passage in question, which I here subjoin:—

"Athalepakapakshanirasartham aha | *Buddhadvaitasatattvasya yatheshtacharanam yadi* | *sunam tattvadrisam chaiva ko bhedo 'suchibhakshane* || 60 || *Kasmanna bhavati yasmat* | *Adharmajjayate 'jnanam yatheshtacharanam tatah* | *dharmakarye katham tat syadyatra dharmopi neshyate* || 61 || . . . *Tishthatu tavat sarvapravrittibijaghasmaram jnanam, mumukshvavasthayam api na sambhavati yatheshtacharanam* | *Tadaha* | *Yo hi yatra viraktah syannasau tasmai pravarttate* | *lokatrayaviraktatwan mumukshuh kimitihate* || 63 ||

The other half couplet, however, of our text, which, be it observed, is *not* Suresvara's, seems to reverse this teaching, and to inculcate the doctrine that the knower of Brahma *may* act as he likes with impunity. I fear that this is really the drift of much of the pantheistic teaching of India, and my opinion is supported by a learned Indian writer, already quoted, who says that "Vedantic authors have boldly asserted that they are subject to no law, no rule, and that there is no such thing as virtue or vice, injunction or prohibition."[3]

1 *Aphorisms*, i. 18. 2 *Rational Refutation*, pp. 30, 31 (*note*).
3 *Dialogues on Hindu Philosophy*, p. 381.

That there are many passages in the Upanishads and elsewhere which teach this, the accompanying extract from an article by Professor Gough will show:—"The Theosophist liberated from metempsychosis, but still in the body, is untouched by merit and demerit, absolved from all works good and evil, unsoiled by sinful works,[1] uninjured by what he has done and by what he has left undone.[2] Good works, like evil works, and like the God that recompenses them, belong to the unreal, to the fictitious duality, the world of semblances. 'Gnosis, once arisen,' says Sankaracharya in his prolegomena to the Svetasvatara, 'requires nothing farther for the realisation of its result, it needs *subsidia* only that it may arise.' Anandagiri:—'The theosophist, so long as he lives, may do good and evil as he chooses and incur no stain, such is the efficiency of gnosis.' And so in the *Taittiriya Upanishad* (ii. 9) we read—'The thought afflicts not him, What good have I felt undone, what evil done?' And in the *Brihadaranyaka*[3]—'Here the thief is no more a thief, the Chandala no more a Chandala, the Paulkasa no more a Paulkasa, the sacred mendicant no more a sacred mendicant: they are not followed by evil works. For at last the sage has passed beyond all the sorrows of his heart.' Immoral inferences from this doctrine—the quietists of all ages have been taxed with immorality—are thus redargued by Nrisimhasarasvati:—'Some one may say, It will follow from this the theosophist may act as he chooses. That he can act as he pleases cannot be denied in the presence of texts of revelation, traditionary texts, and arguments such as the following: 'Not by matricide, not by parricide.' 'He that does not identify not-self with self, whose inner faculty is unsullied,—he, though he slay these people, neither slays them, nor is slain.' . . . 'He that knows the truth is sullied neither by good actions nor by evil actions,' . . . In answer to all this we reply: True, but as these texts are only eulogistic of the theosophist; it is not intended that he should thus act.'[4]

The line of argument adopted by this commentator, and also by other apologists, is unsafe, and does not get rid of the fact that some of the Upanishads, the chief source of the Vedanta doctrine, do, without any qualification, declare that sin and virtue are alike to one who knows Brahma; and the system is therefore rightly charged with immorality. But, independently of such teaching as this, what moral results could possibly be expected from a system so devoid of motives for a life of true purity? The Supreme Being, Brahma, is a cold Impersonality, out of relation with the world, unconscious of His own esixtence and of ours, and devoid of all attributes and qualities. The so-called personal God, the first manifestation of the Impersonal, turns out on examination to be a myth; there is no God apart from ourselves, no Creator, no Holy Being, no Father, no Judge—no one, in a word, to adore, to love, or to fear. And as for ourselves, we are only unreal actors on the semblance of a stage!

1 *Brihaddranyakopanishad,* 4. 4. 23. 2 *Ibid.,* 4. 4. 22.
3 *Brihadaranyakopanishad,* 4. 3. 22.
4 *Calcutta Review* (1878), p. 34.

The goal, already referred to, is worthy of such a creed, being no less than the complete extinction of all spiritual, mental, and bodily powers by absorption into the Impersonal.

"Annihilation, then, as regards individuals, is as much the ultimate destiny of the soul as it is of the body, and *'Not to be'* is the melancholy result of the religion and philosophy of the Hindus."[1]

5. *'He already free, is freed.'*

"Though illusion has not really real existence, yet it possesses apparent existence, and so it is capable of taking the soul captive. And again, the Vedantins say, that as illusion is only apparent, so the soul's being fattered is practical; that is, as illusion is false, so the soul's being fattered is likewise false. Neither was the soul ever actually fettered, nor is it now fettered, nor has it to be emancipated."[2]

This matter is also explained in the last chapter of the *Vedanta-paribhasha*:—"The joy which admits of no increase, is Brahma; as the Veda says, 'He knew Brahma to be joy.' The acquisition of Brahma, whose essence is joy, is *moksha,* and it is also the cessation of sorrow; as the Veda says, 'The knower of Brahma becomes Brahma,' and again, 'The knower of Self passes beyond sorrow.' The acquisition of another world, or the sensuous joy derivable therefrom, is not *moksha;* for as it is the result of works, and therefore non-eternal, the subject of such liberation is liable to future births. If you say that, as, even according to our view, the acquisition of bliss and the cessation of misery have a beginning, they are therefore cheargeable with the same defect [*i.e.,* of being non-eternal and therefore transitory], I reply, Not so; for, although *moksha,* consisting of Brahma, is already in possession, still, because of the erroneous idea that it is not possessed, it is proper to make use of means for attaining it. The cessation of misery, too, in the form of Brahma, who is the substrate of all, is already an accomplished fact. Even in mundane affairs, however, we see the need of obtaining things already obtained, and of removing things already removed. For example, when a piece of gold is in one's hand, but has been forgotten [and is being searched for], and some person says, 'Why, the gold is in your hand,' one regains it as if it had not already been in possession. So, too, in the case of one who is under the delusion that the garland encircling his ankle is a snake; when a reliable person tells him that it is not a snake, the snake is removed although it was already removed [*i.e.,* had never existed]. In like manner, the acquisition of a joy already possessed, and the cessation of misery already removed, in other words, *liberation,* is an object [to be sought after]."

1 Wilson's *Essays on the Religion of the Hindus,* ii. 114.
2 *Rational Refutation,* p. 189.

REFERENCES

Dialogues on the Hindu Philosophy. K. M. Banerjee, 1861.

A Rational Refutation of the Hindu Philosophical Systems. By Nehemiah Nilakantha Sastri Gore. Translated by Fitzedward Hall, 1862.

Miscellaneous Essays. H. T. Colebrooke. With Notes by Professor Cowell, 1873.

The Philosophy of the Upanishads. A. E. Gough, 1878.

Original Sanskrit Texts. J. Muir, vols. iii.-v.

Sacred Books of the East. Ed. by Max Muller, vol. i., *Upanishads,* 1879.

H. H. Wilson's Works:—(a) *Essays on the Religion of the Hindus,* 2 vols. Ed. by Rost, 1862. (b) *Essays on Sanskrit Literature,* 3 vols. Ed. by Rost, 1864-65. (c) *Vishnu Purana,* 6 vols. Ed. by Fitzedward Hall, 1864-77.

The History of Indian Literature. Weber, translated from the second German edition, 1878.

The Indian Antiquary, vols. i, ii., and iv. Bombay, 1872, 1873, 1875.

Anti- Theistic Theories, the Baird Lecture for 1877. R. Flint, 1879.

Works by R. Spence Hardy: (a) *Eastern Monachism,* 1860. (b) *Legends and Theories of the Buddhists,* 1866. (c) *Manual of Buddhism,* 2nd edition, 1880.

Elphinstone's *History of India,* 6th edition. E. B. Cowell, 1874.

Works by Dr. Ballantyne: (a) *The Sankhya Aphorisms of Kapila,* translated. Bibliotheca Indica Series, 1865. (b) *The Aphorisms of the Yoga Philosophy,* Book I., translated, 1852. (c) *The Aphorisms of the Nyaya Philosophy,* translated, 1850. (d) *A Lecture on the Vedanta,* 1850.

The Aphorisms of Sandilya. Translated by Cowell. Bibliotheca Indica Series, 1878.

The History of Philosophy. G. H. Lewes, 2 vols., Longmans, 1871.

Panchadasi. Bharatitirthavidyaranya, 1879.

Upadesasahasri. Sankaracharya. Published in "*The Pandit.*" Benares, 1868-69.

Adhyatma-Ramayana. Calcutta, 1872.

Aitareya Brahmana. Ed. and tr. by Haug, 2 vols.

Sankhyapravachanabhashya. Ed. by Jibananda Vidyasagara Calcutta.

Kavya Prakasha. Ed. by Mahesa Chandra Nyayaratna, 1866.

Hastamalaka. Bound up with Jibananda's edition of Vedantasara.

Vakyasudha. By Sankaracharya. Ed. by Windischmann in 1833 under the erroneous title of *Balabodhini.* (*Vide* Hall's *"Contribution towards an Index to the Bibliography of Indian Philosophical Systems."*)

Naishkarmyasiddhi. By Sureswaracharya. MSS. No. 1103 and 777 in India Office Library.

Patanjaladarsana. Ed. by Jibananda Vidyasagara. Calcutta 1874.

Sankhyasara. Edited by Fitzedward Hall. Calcutta, 1862 (Bibliotheca Indica Series.)

Upanishads

Kaushitaki and *Maitri.* Edited and translated by Cowell, 1861 and 1870.

Kena, Katha Mundaka, Mandukya, Chhandogya, Taittiriya Aitareya, Svetasvatara, and *Brihadaranyaka.* Edited by Jibananda Vidyasagara at Calcutta. They are facsimiles of those brought out in the Bibliotheca Indica Series.

Muktika. Edited by Jibananda Vidyasagara.

वेदान्तसारः ।

अखण्डं सच्चिदानन्दमवाङ्मनसगोचरम् ।
आत्मानमखिलाधारमाश्रयेऽभीष्टसिद्धये ॥ १ ॥
अर्थतोऽप्यद्वयानन्दानतीतद्वैतभानतः ।
गुरूनाराध्य वेदान्त-सारं वक्ष्ये यथामति ॥ २ ॥

वेदान्तो नाम,—उपनिषत्प्रमाणं, तदुपकारीणि शारीरकसूत्रादीनि च ॥ ३ ॥

अस्य वेदान्तप्रकरणत्वात् तदीयैरेवानुबन्धैः तद्वत्तासिद्धेर्न ते पृथगालोचनीयाः ॥ ४ ॥

तत्रानुबन्धो नाम,—अधिकारिविषयसम्बन्धप्रयोजनानि ॥ ५ ॥

अधिकारी तु,—विधिवदधीतवेदवेदाङ्गत्वेन आपाततोऽधिगताखिलवेदार्थः, अस्मिन् जन्मनि जन्मान्तरे वा काम्यनिषिद्धवर्जनपुरःसरं नित्यनैमित्तिकप्रायश्चित्तोपासनाऽनुष्ठानेन निर्गतनिखिलकल्मषतया नितान्तनिर्मलस्वान्तः, साधनचतुष्टयसम्पन्नः प्रमाता ॥ ६ ॥

काम्यानि,—स्वर्गादीष्टसाधनानि ज्योतिष्टोमादीनि ॥ ७ ॥

निषिद्धानि,—नरकाद्यनिष्टसाधनानि ब्रह्महननादीनि ॥ ८ ॥

नित्यानि,—अकरणे प्रत्यवायसाधनानि सन्ध्यावन्दनादीनि ॥ ९ ॥

नैमित्तिकानि,—पुत्रजन्माद्यनुबन्धानि जातेष्ट्यादीनि ॥ १० ॥

प्रायश्चित्तानि,—पापक्षयमात्रसाधनानि चान्द्रायणादीनि ॥ ११ ॥

उपासनानि,—सगुणब्रह्मविषयकमानसव्यापाररूपाणि शाण्डिल्यविद्यादीनि ॥ १२ ॥

एतेषां नित्यादीनां बुद्धिशुद्धिः परं प्रयोजनम्; उपासनानान्तु चित्तैका-

ग्रग्रम्। "तमेतं वेदानुवचनेन ब्राह्मणा विविदिषन्ति यज्ञेन" [वृह० ४ अ० ४ ब्रा० २२ मन्त्रः] इत्यादिश्रुतेः, "तपसा कल्मषं हन्ति विद्ययाऽमृतमश्नुते" [मनु० १२ अ० १०४ श्लोकः] इत्यादि स्मृतेश्च ॥ १३ ॥

नित्यनैमित्तिकयोरुपासनानाञ्च अवान्तरफलं पितृलोकसत्यलोकप्राप्तिः "कर्म्मणा पितृलोको विद्यया देवलोकः" [वृह० १ अध्या० ५ ब्रा० १६ मन्त्रः] इत्यादिश्रुतेः ॥ १४ ॥

साधनानि,—नित्यानित्यवस्तुविवेक इहामुत्रफलभोगविराग-शमदमादिसम्पत्ति मुमुक्षुत्वानि ॥ १५ ॥

नित्यानित्यवस्तुविवेकस्तावत्,—ब्रह्मैव नित्यं वस्तु, ततोऽन्यदखिलमनित्यमिति विवेचनम् ।१६ ॥

ऐहिकानां स्रक्चन्दनवनितादि विषयभोगाणां कर्म्मजन्यतया अनित्यत्ववत् आमुष्मिकाणामपि अमृतादिविषयभोगाणामनित्यतया तेभ्यो नितरां विरतिः, इहामुत्रफलभोगविरागः ॥ १७ ॥

शमदमादयस्तु—शम-दम-उपरति-तितिक्षासमाधान-श्रद्धाख्याः ॥ १८ ॥

शमस्तावत्—श्रवणादिव्यतिरिक्तविषयेभ्यो मनसो निग्रहः ॥ १९ ॥

दमः,—वाह्यविषयेन्द्रियाणां तद्व्यतिरिक्तविषयेभ्यो निवर्त्तनम् ॥ २० ॥

निवर्त्तितानामेतेषां तद्व्यतिरिक्तविषयेभ्यः उपरमणम्, उपरतिः; अथवा विहितानां कर्म्मणां विधिना परित्यागः ॥ २१ ॥

तितिक्षा—शीतोष्णादिद्वन्द्वसहिष्णुता ॥ २२ ॥

निगृहीतस्य मनसः श्रवणादौ तदनुगुणविषये च समाधिः समाधानम् ॥ २३ ।

गुरुवेदान्तादिवाक्येषु विश्वासः श्रद्धा ॥ २४ ॥

मुमुक्षुत्वं—मोक्षेच्छा ॥ २५ ॥

एवम्भूतः प्रमाता अधिकारी। "शान्तो दान्तः" [वृह० ४ अध्या० ४ ब्रा० २३ मन्त्रः] इत्यादिश्रुतेः। उक्तञ्च,—"प्रशान्तचित्ताय जितेन्द्रियाय च

प्रहीणदोषाय यथोक्तकारिणे। गुणान्विताया्ऽनुगताय सर्व्वदा प्रदेयमेतत् सकलं मुमुक्षवे ॥" इति [उपदेशसाहस्रा ४१६ श्लोकः] ॥ २६ ॥

विषयः,—जीवब्रह्मैक्यं शुद्धचैतन्यं प्रमेयं, तत्रैव वेदान्तानां तात्पर्य्यात् ॥ २७ ॥

सम्बन्धस्तु—तदैक्यप्रमेयस्य तत्प्रतिपादकोपनिषत्प्रमाणस्य च बोध्यबोधकभावः ॥ २८ ॥

प्रयोजनन्तु—तदैक्यप्रमेयगताज्ञाननिवृत्तिः, तत्स्वरूपानन्दावाप्तिश्च। "तरति शोकमात्मावत्" [छान्दो० ७अ० १खण्ड० ३मन्त्रः] इति श्रुतेः "ब्रह्म वेद ब्रह्मैव भवति" [मुण्ड० ३ मुण्ड० २ खण्ड० ९ मन्त्रः] इत्यादिश्रुतेश्च ॥ २९

अयमधिकारी जननमरणादिसंसारानलसन्तप्तो दीप्तशिरा जलराशिमिव उपहारपाणिः श्रोत्रियं ब्रह्मनिष्ठं गुरुमुपसृत्य तमनुसरति। "समित्पाणिः श्रोत्रियं ब्रह्मनिष्ठम्" [मुण्ड० १ मुण्ड० २ खण्ड० १२ मन्त्रः] इत्यादिश्रुतेः ॥ ३० ॥

स परमकृपया अध्यारोपापवादन्यायेन एनमुपदिशति। "तस्मै स विद्वानुपसन्नाय सम्यक् प्रशान्तचित्ताय शमान्विताय। येनाक्षरं पुरुषं वेद सत्यं प्रावाच तं तत्त्वतो ब्रह्मविद्याम्" [मुण्ड० १ मुण्ड० २ खण्ड० १३ मन्त्रः] इत्यादिश्रुतेः ॥ ३१ ॥

असर्पभूतायां रज्जौ सर्पारोपवत् वस्तुनि अवस्त्वारोपः अध्यारोपः ॥ ३२ ॥

वस्तु—सच्चिदानन्दमद्वयं ब्रह्म ॥ ३३ ॥

अज्ञानादिसकलजड़समूहः अवस्तु ॥ ३४ ॥

अज्ञानन्तु—सदसद्भ्याम् अनिर्वचनीयं, त्रिगुणात्मकं ज्ञानविरोधि भावरूपं यत्किञ्चिदिति वदन्ति। अहमज्ञ इत्याद्यनुभवात्, "देवात्मशक्तिं स्वगुणैर्निगूढ़ाम्" [श्वेता० १ अध्या० ३ मन्त्रः] इत्तादिश्रुतेश्च ॥ ३५ ॥

इदमज्ञानं समष्टिव्यष्टयभिप्रायेणैकमनेकमिति च व्यवह्रियते ॥ ३६ ॥

तथाहि यथा वृक्षाणां समष्टयभिप्रायेण वनमित्येकत्वव्यपदेशः, यथा वा जलानां समष्टयभिप्रायेण जलाशय इति, तथा नानात्वेन प्रतिभासमानानां जावगताज्ञानानां समष्टयभिप्रायेण तदेकत्वव्यपदेशः, "अजामेकाम्" [श्वेता० ४ अध्या० ५ मन्त्रः] इत्यादिश्रुतेः ॥ ३७ ॥

इयं समष्टिरुत्कृष्टोपाधितया विशुद्धसत्त्वप्रधाना ; एतदुपहितं चैतन्यं सर्व्वज्ञत्वसर्व्वेश्वरत्वसर्व्वनियन्तृत्वादिगुणकमव्यक्तमन्तर्य्यामी जगत् कारणमीश्वर इति च व्यपदिश्यते ॥ ३८ ॥

सकलाज्ञानावभासकत्वादस्य सर्व्वज्ञत्वम् । "यः सर्व्वज्ञः सर्व्ववित्" [मुण्ड० १ मुण्ड० १ खण्ड० ९ मन्त्रः] इति श्रुतेः ॥ ३९ ॥

अस्येयं ममष्टिरखिलकारणत्वात् कारणशरीरम्, आनन्दप्रचुरत्वात् कोषवदाच्छादकत्वाच्च आनन्दमयकोषः, सर्वोपरमत्वात् सुषुप्तिः, अत एव स्थूलसूक्ष्मप्रपञ्चलयस्थानमिति चोच्यते ॥ ४० ॥

यथा वनस्य व्यष्टयभिप्रायेण वृक्षा इत्यनेकत्वव्यपदेशः, यथा वा जलाशयस्य व्यष्टयभिप्रायेण जलानीति, तथाऽज्ञानस्य व्यष्टयभिप्रायेण तदनेकत्वव्यपदेशः। "इन्द्रो मायाभिः पुरुरूप ईयते" इत्यादिश्रुतेः ॥ ४१ ॥

अत्र व्यस्तसमस्तव्यापित्वेन व्यष्टिसमष्टिताव्यपदेशः ॥ ४२ ॥

इयं व्यष्टिर्निकृष्टापाधितया मलिनसत्त्वप्रधाना ॥ ४३ ॥

एतदुपहितं चैतन्यमल्पज्ञत्वानीश्वरत्वादिगुणकं प्राज्ञ इत्युच्यते ॥ ४४ ॥

एकाज्ञानावभासकत्वादस्य प्राज्ञत्वम्, अस्पष्टोपाधितयाऽनतिप्रकाशकत्वम् ॥ ४५ ॥

अस्यापीयमहङ्कारादिकारणत्वात् कारणशरीरम्, आनन्दप्रचुरत्वात् कोषवदाच्छादकत्वाच्च आनन्दमयकोषः, सर्व्वोपरमत्वात् सुषुप्तिः, अत एव स्थूलसूक्ष्मशरीरप्रपञ्चलयस्थानमिति चोच्यते ॥ ४६ ॥

तदानीमेतौ ईश्वरप्राज्ञौ चैतन्यप्रदीप्ताभिः अतिसूक्ष्माभिरज्ञानवृत्तिभिः आनन्दमनुभवतः। "आनन्दभुक् चेतो मुखः प्राज्ञः" [माण्डु० ५ मन्त्रः] इत्यादिश्रुतेः, सुखमहमस्वाप्सं न किञ्चिदवेदिषमित्युत्थितस्य परामर्शोपपत्तेश्च ।। ४७ ।।

अनयोः समष्टिव्यष्ट्योर्वनवृक्षयोरिव जलाशयजलयोरिव चाभेदः ।। ४८ ।।

एतदुपहितयोरीश्वरप्राज्ञयोरपि वनवृक्षावच्छिन्नाकाशयोरिव जलाशयजलगतप्रतिबिम्बाकाशयोरिव चाभेदः। "एष सर्वेश्वर एष सर्वज्ञ एषोऽन्तर्य्याम्येष योनिः सर्वस्य प्रभवाप्ययौ हि भूतानाम्" [माण्डु० ६ मन्त्रः] इत्यादि श्रुतेः ।। ४९ ।।

वनवृक्षतदवच्छिन्नाकाशयोर्जलाशयजलगतप्रतिबिम्बाकाशोर्वा आधारभूतानुपहिताकाशवदनयोरज्ञानतदुपहितचैतन्ययोराधारभूतं यदनुपहितं चैतन्यं तत् तुरीयमित्युच्यते। "शान्तं शिवमद्वैतं चतुर्थं मन्यन्ते स आत्मा स विज्ञेयः" [माण्डु० ७ मन्त्रः] इत्यादिश्रुतेः ।। ५० ।।

इदमेव तुरीयं शुद्धचैतन्यमज्ञानादितदुपहितचैतन्याभ्यां तप्तायःपिण्डवदविविक्तं सन्महावाक्यस्य वाच्यं, विविक्तं सल्लक्ष्यमिति चोच्यते ।। ५१ ।।

अस्याज्ञानस्यावरणविक्षेपनामकमस्ति शक्तिद्वयम् ॥ ५२ ॥

आवरणशक्तिस्तावदल्पोऽपि मेघाऽनेकयोजनाऽऽयतमादित्यमण्डलमवलोकयितृनयनपथपिधायकतया यथाऽऽच्छादयतीव, तथाऽज्ञानं परिच्छिन्नमप्यात्मानमपरिच्छिन्नमसंसारिणमवलोकयितृबुद्धिपिधायकतयाऽऽच्छादयतीव तादृशं सामर्थ्यम्। तदुक्तं—"घनच्छन्नदृष्टिर्घनच्छन्नमर्कं यथा निष्प्रभं मन्यते चातिमूढः। तथा बद्धवद्भाति यो मूढदृष्टेः स नित्योपलब्धिस्वरूपोऽहमात्मा ॥" इत्यादि [हस्ता० १० श्लोकः] ।। ५३ ।।

अनयैवावरणशक्त्यावच्छिन्नस्यात्मनः कर्तृत्वभोक्तृत्वसुखित्वदुःखित्वादिमोहात्मकतुच्छसंसारभावनाऽपि सम्भाव्यते, यथा स्वाज्ञानेन आवृतायां रज्ज्वां सर्पत्वसम्भावना ।। ५४ ।।

विक्षेपशक्तिस्तु—यथा रज्ज्वज्ञानं स्वावृतरज्जौ स्वशक्त्या सर्पादिकमुद्भावयति, एवमज्ञानमपि स्वावृतात्मनि विक्षेपशक्त्या आकाशादिप्रपञ्चमुद्भावयति तादृशं सामर्थ्यम्। तदुक्तम् "विक्षेपशक्तिर्लिङ्गादिब्रह्माण्डान्तं जगत् सृजेत्" [वाक्यसुधा १३] इति ॥ ५५ ॥

शक्तिद्वयवदज्ञानोपहितं चैतन्यं स्वप्रधानतया निमित्तं स्वोपाधिप्रधानतयोपादानञ्च भवति, यथा लूता तन्तुकार्य्यं प्रति स्वप्रधानतया निमित्तं, स्वशरीरप्रधानतयोपादानञ्च भवति ॥ ५६ ॥

तमःप्रधानविक्षेपशक्तिमदज्ञानोपहितचैतन्यादाकाशः, आकाशाद्वायुः, वायोरग्निः, अग्नेरापः, अद्भ्यः पृथिवी चोत्पद्यते। "तस्माद्वा एतस्मादात्मन आकाशः सम्भूतः" [तैत्ति० उप० २ वल्ली० १ अनु०] इत्यादिश्रुतेः" ॥ ५७ ॥

तेषु जाड्याधिक्यदर्शनात् तमः प्राधान्यं तत्कारणस्य ॥ ५८ ॥

तदानीं सत्त्वरजस्तमांसि कारणगुणप्रक्रमेण तेषु आकाशादिषु उत्पद्यन्ते ॥ ५९ ॥

इमानि एव सूक्ष्मभूतानि तन्मात्राणि अपञ्चीकृतानि चोच्यन्ते ॥ ६० ॥

एतेभ्यः सूक्ष्मशरीराणि स्थूलभूतानि चोत्पद्यन्ते; सुक्ष्मशरीराणि—सप्तदशावयवानि लिङ्गशरीराणि ॥ ६१ ॥

अवयवास्तु—ज्ञानेन्द्रियपञ्चकं बुद्धिमनसी कर्मेन्द्रियपञ्चकं वायुपञ्चकञ्चेति ॥ ६२ ॥

ज्ञानेन्द्रियाणि—श्रोत्रत्वक्चक्षुर्जिह्वाघ्राणाख्यानि ॥ ६३ ॥

एतान्याकाशादीनां सात्त्विकांशेभ्यो व्यस्तेभ्यः पृथक् पृथक् क्रमेणोत्पद्यन्ते ॥ ६४ ॥

बुद्धिर्नाम—निश्चयात्मिका अन्तःकरणवृत्तिः।

मनो नाम—सङ्कल्प-विकल्पात्मिका अन्तःकरणवृत्तिः ॥ ६५ ॥

अनयोरेव चित्ताहङ्कारयोरन्तर्भावः। अनुसन्धानात्मिका अन्तःकरणवृत्तिः, चित्तम्। अभिमानात्मिका अन्तःकरणवृत्तिः, अहङ्कारः ॥ ६६ ॥

एते पुनराकाशादिगतसात्त्विकांशेभ्यो मिलितेभ्य उत्पद्यन्ते। एतेषां प्रकाशात्मकत्त्वात् सात्त्विकांशकार्य्यत्वम् ॥ ६७ ॥

इयं बुद्धिर्ज्ञानेन्द्रियैः सहिता सती, विज्ञानमयकोषो भवति ॥ ६८ ॥

अयं कर्तृत्वभोक्तृत्वसुखित्वदुःखित्वाद्यभिमानत्वेन इहलोकपरलोकगामी व्यावहारिको जीव इत्युच्यते ॥ ६९ ॥

मनस्तु ज्ञानेन्द्रियैः सहितं सन्मनोमयकोषो भवति ॥ ७० ॥

कर्मेन्द्रियाणि—वाक्पाणपादपायूपस्थाख्यानि। एतानि पुनराकाशादीनां रजोऽंशेभ्यो व्यस्तेभ्यः पृथक् पृथक क्रमेण उत्पद्यन्ते ॥ ७१ ॥

वायवः,—प्राणापानव्यानोदानसमानाः ॥ ७२ ॥

प्राणो नाम—प्राग्गमनवान् नासाग्रस्थानवर्त्ती ॥ ७३ ॥

अपानो नाम—अवाग्गमनवान् पाय्वादिस्थानवर्त्ती ॥ ७४ ॥

व्यानो नाम—विश्वग्गमनवान् अखिलशरीरवर्त्ती ॥ ७५ ॥

उदानो नाम—कण्ठस्थानीय ऊर्द्ध्वगमनवान् उत्क्रमणवायुः ॥ ७६ ॥

समानो नाम—शरीरमध्यगताशितपीतान्नादिसमीकरण करः। समीकरणन्तु—परिपाककरणं रसरुधिरशुक्रपुरीषादिकरणम् ॥ ७७ ॥

केचित्तु नागकुर्मकृकरदेवदत्तधनञ्जयाख्याः पञ्च अन्ये वायवः सन्तीत्याहुः ॥ ७८ ॥

तत्र नागः, उद्गिरणकरः। कूर्मः,—उन्मीलनकरः। कृकरः,—क्षुधाकरः। देवदत्तः,—जृम्भणकरः। धनञ्जयः,—पोषणकरः ॥ ७९ ॥

एतेषां प्राणादिषु अन्तर्भावात् प्राणादयः पञ्च एव इति केचित् ॥ ८० ॥

एतत्प्राणादिपञ्चकम् आकाशादिगतरजोऽंशेभ्यो मिलितेभ्य उत्पद्यते ॥ ८१ ॥

इदं प्राणादिपञ्चकं कर्मेन्द्रियैः सहितं सत् प्राणमयकोषो भवति ॥ ८२ ॥

अस्य क्रियात्मकत्वेन रजोऽंशकार्य्यत्वम् ॥ ८३ ॥

एतेषु कोषेषु मध्ये विज्ञानमया ज्ञानशक्तिमान् कर्तृरूपः ; मनोमय इच्छाशक्तिमान् करणरूप; प्रानमयः क्रियाशक्तिमान् कार्य्यरूपः; योग्यत्वादेवमेतेषां विभाग इति वर्णयन्ति ॥ ८४ ॥

एतत् कौषत्रयं मिलितं सत् सूक्ष्मशरीरमित्युच्यते ॥ ८५ ॥

अत्रापि अखिलसूक्ष्मशरीरम् एकबुद्धिविषयतया वनवज्जलाशयवद्वा समष्टिः, अनेकबुद्धिविषयतया वृक्षवज्जलवद्वा व्यष्टिश्च भवति ॥ ८६ ॥

एतत्समष्ट्युपहितं चैतन्यं सूत्रात्मा, हिरण्यगर्भः, प्राण इति चोच्यते, सर्वत्रानुस्यूतत्वात् ज्ञानेच्छाक्रियाशक्तिमदुपहितत्वाच्च ॥ ८७ ॥

अस्यैषा समष्टिः स्थूलप्रपञ्चापेक्षया सूक्ष्मत्वात् सूक्ष्मशरीरं विज्ञानमयादिकोषत्रयं, जाग्रद्वासनामयत्वात् स्वप्नः, अत एव स्थूलप्रपञ्चलयस्थानमिति चोच्यते ॥ ८८ ॥

एतद्व्यष्ट्युपहितं चैतन्यं तैजसो भवति, तेजोमयान्तःकरणोपहितत्वात् ॥ ८९ ॥

अस्यापि इयं व्यष्टिः स्थूलशरीरपेक्षया सुक्ष्मत्वात् सूक्ष्मशरीरं विज्ञानमयादिकोषत्रयं, जाग्रद्वासनामयत्वात् स्वप्नः, अत एव स्थूलशरीरलयस्थानमिति चोच्यते ॥ ९० ॥

एतौ सूत्रात्मतैजसौ तदानीं सूक्ष्माभिर्मनोवृत्तिभिः सूक्ष्मविषयान् अनुभवतः "प्रविविक्तभुक् तैजसः" [माण्डू० ४] इत्यादिश्रुतेः ॥ ९१ ॥

अत्रापि समष्टिव्यष्ट्योस्तदुपहितसूत्रात्मतैजमयोः वनवृक्षवत् तदवच्छिन्नाकाशवच्च जलाशयजलवत् तद्गतप्रतिबिम्बाकाशवच्चाभेदः ॥ ९२ ॥

एवं सूक्ष्मशरीरोत्पत्तिः ॥ ९३ ॥

स्थूलभुतानि तु पञ्चीकृतानि ॥ ९४ ॥

पञ्चीकरणन्तु आकाशादिपञ्चसु एकैकं द्विधा समं विभज्य, तेषु दशसु

भागेषु प्राथमिकान् पञ्च भागान् प्रत्येकं चतुर्धा समं विभज्य, तेषां चतूर्णां भागानां स्वस्वद्वितीयार्द्धभागं परित्यज्य, भागान्तरेषु संयोजनम्। तदुक्तं,—"द्विधा विधाय चैकैकं चतुर्धा प्रथमं पुनः। स्वस्वेतरद्वितीयांशैर्योजनात् पञ्च पञ्च ते ॥" इति [पञ्चदशी १ पार० २७ श्लोकः] ॥ ९५ ॥

अस्याप्रामाण्यं नाशङ्कनीयं, त्रिवृत्करणश्रुते पञ्चीकरणस्याप्युपलक्षणार्थत्वात् ॥ ९६ ॥

पञ्चानां पञ्चात्मकत्वे समानेऽपि तेषु च "वैशेष्यात्तु तद्वादस्तद्वादः" [ब्रह्मसूत्र० २ अध्यां० ४ पाद० २२ सूत्रम्] इति न्यायेन आकाशादिव्यपदेशः सम्भवति ॥ ९७ ॥

तदानीमाकाशे शब्दोऽभिव्यज्यते, वायौ शब्दस्पर्शौ, अग्नौ शब्दस्पर्शरूपाणि, अप्सु शब्दस्पर्शरूपरसाः पृथिव्यां शब्दस्पर्शरूपरसगन्धाश्च ॥ ९८ ॥

एतेभ्यः पञ्चीकृतेभ्यो भूतेभ्यो भूर्भुवः स्वर्महर्जनस्तपः सत्यमित्येतन्नामकानामुपर्य्युपरि विद्यमानानाम् अतलवितलसुतलरसातलतलातलमहातलपातालनामकानामधोऽधोविद्यमामानानां लोकानां ब्रह्माण्डस्य, तदन्तर्गतचतुर्विधस्थूलशरीराणां तदुचितानामन्नपानादीनाञ्चोत्पत्तिर्भवति ॥ ९९ ॥

चतुर्विधस्थूलशरीराणि—जरायुजाण्डजस्वेदजोद्भिज्जाख्यानि ॥ १०० ॥

जरायुजानि—जरायुभ्यो जातानि मनुष्यपश्वादीनि ॥ १०१ ॥

अण्डजानि—अण्डेभ्यो जातानि पक्षिपन्नगादीनि ॥ १०२ ॥

स्वेदजानि—स्वेदेभ्यो जातानि यूकमशकादीनि ॥ १०३ ॥

उद्भिज्जानि—भूमिमुद्भिद्य जातानि लतावृक्षादीनि ॥ १०४ ॥

अत्रापि चतुर्विधस्थूलशरीरम् एकानेकबुद्धिविषयतया वनवज्जलाशयवद्वा समष्टिः, वृक्षवज्जलवद्वा व्यष्टिरपि भवति ॥ १०५ ॥

एतत् समष्ट्युपहितं चैतन्यं वैश्वानरो विराडिति चोच्यते, सर्वनराभिमानित्वाद् विविधं राजमानत्वाच्च ॥ १०६ ॥

अस्यैषा समष्टिः स्थूलरीरम्, अन्नविकारत्वादन्नमयकोषः, स्थूलभोगायतनत्वाच्च स्थूलशरीरं जाग्रदिति च व्यपदिश्यते ॥ १०७ ॥

एतद्व्यष्ट्युपहितं चैतन्यं विश्व इत्युच्यते, सूक्ष्मशरीराभिमानमपरित्यज्य स्थूलशरीरादिप्रवेष्टृत्वात् ॥ १०८ ॥

अस्याप्येषा व्यष्टिः स्थूलशरीरम्, अन्नविकारत्वाद् एव हेतोः अन्नमयकोषः, स्तूलभोगायतनत्वाद् स्थूलशरीरं जाग्रदिति चोच्यते ॥ १०९ ॥

तदानीमेतौ विश्ववैश्वानरौ, दिग्वातार्कप्रचेतोऽश्विभिः क्रमान्नियन्त्रितेन श्रोत्रादीन्द्रियपञ्चकेन क्रमाच्छब्दस्पर्शरूपरसगन्धान् ॥ ११० ॥

अग्नीन्द्रोपेन्द्रयमप्रजापतिभिः क्रमान्नियन्त्रितेन वागादिन्द्रियपञ्चकेन क्रमाद्वचनादानगमनविसर्गानन्दान् ॥ १११ ॥

चन्द्रचतुर्मुखशङ्कराच्युतैः क्रमान्नियन्त्रितेन मनोबुद्ध्यहङ्कारचिताख्येन अन्तरिन्द्रियचतुष्केण क्रमात् सङ्कल्पनिश्चयाहङ्कार्य्यचैत्तांश्च सर्वानेतान् स्थूलविषयाननुभवतः "जागरितस्थानो वहिःप्रज्ञः" [माण्डु० ३] इत्यादिश्रुतेः ॥ ११२ ॥

अत्राप्यनयोः स्थूलव्यष्टिसमष्ट्योस्तदुपहितयोर्विश्ववैश्वानरयोश्च वनवृक्षवत् तदवच्छिन्नाकाशवच्च जलाशयजलवत् तद्गतप्रतिविम्बाकाशवच्च वा पूर्ववदभेदः ॥ ११३ ॥

एवं पञ्चीकृतपञ्चीभूतेभ्यः स्थूलप्रपञ्चोत्पत्तिः ॥ ११४ ॥

एषां स्थूलसूक्ष्मकारणप्रपञ्चानामपि समष्टिरेको महान् प्रपञ्चो भवति, यथा अवान्तरवनानां समष्टिरेकं महद्वनं भवति, यथा वा अवान्तरजलाशयानां समष्टिरेको महान् जलाशयः ॥ ११५ ॥

एतदुपहितं विश्ववैश्वानरादीश्वरपर्य्यन्तं चैतन्यमपि अवान्तरवनावच्छिन्नाकाशवद् अवान्तरजलाशयगतप्रतिविम्बाकाशवच्च एकमेव ॥ ११६ ॥

आभ्यां महाप्रपञ्चतदुपहितचैतन्याभ्यां तप्तायःपिण्डवदविविक्तं सद्

अनुपहितं चैतन्यं "सर्वं खल्विदं ब्रह्म" [छान्दो० ३ अध्या० १४ खण्ड० १ मन्त्रः] इति महावाक्यस्य वाच्यं भवति, ।वविक्तं सल्लक्ष्यमपि भवा।त ।। ११७ ।।

एवं वस्तुनि अवस्त्वारोपोऽध्यारोपः सामान्येन प्रदर्शितः ।। ११८ ।।

इदानीं प्रत्यगात्मनि इदमिदमयमयमारापयतीति विशेषत उच्यते ।। ११९ ।।

अतिप्राकृतस्तु "आत्मा वै पुत्त्र नामासि" [कौषा० २ अध्या० ११ मन्त्रः] इत्यादिश्रुतेः स्वस्मिन्निव स्वपुत्त्रेऽपि प्रेमदर्शनात्, पुत्त्रे पुष्टे नष्टे चाहमेव पुष्टो नष्टश्चेत्याद्यनुभवाच्च, पुत्त्र आत्मेति वदति ।। १२० ।।

चार्वाकस्तु "स वा एष पुरुषोऽन्नरसमयः" [तैत्ति० उप० २ वल्ली० १ अनु० १ मन्त्रः] इत्यादिश्रुतेः प्रदीप्तगृहात् स्वपुत्त्रं परित्यज्यापि स्वस्य निर्गमदर्शनात् "स्थूलोऽहं" "कृशोऽहम्" इत्याद्यनुभवाच्च, स्थूलशरीरमात्मेति वदति ।। १२१ ।।

अपरश्चार्वाकः "ते ह प्राणाः प्रजापतिं पितरमेत्योचुः" [छान्दो० ५ अध्या० १ खण्ड० ७ मन्त्रः] इत्यादिश्रुतेः इन्द्रियाणामभावे शरीरचलनाभावात् "काणोऽहं" "बधिरोऽहम्" इत्याद्यनुभवाच्च, इन्द्रियाण्यात्मेति वदति । १२२ ।।

अन्यस्तु चार्वाकः "अन्योऽन्तर आत्मा प्राणमयः" [तैत्ति० उप० २ वल्ली० २ अनु०] इत्यादिश्रुते, प्राणाभावे इन्द्रियादिचलनायोगात् "अहमशनायावान्" "अहं पिपासावान्" इत्याद्यनुभवाच्च, प्राण आत्मेति वदति ।। १२३ ।।

अन्यस्तु चार्वाकः "अन्योऽन्तर आत्मा मनोमयः" [तैत्ति० २ वल्ली० ३ अनु०] इत्यादिश्रुतेः मनसि सुप्ते प्राणादेरभावात्, "अहं सङ्कल्पवान्" "अहं विकल्पवान्" इत्याद्यनुभावाच्च, मन आत्मेति वदति ।। १२४ ।।

बौद्धस्तु योऽन्तरआत्मा विज्ञानमयः" [तैत्ति०, २ वल्ली०, ४ अनु०] इत्यादिश्रुतेः कर्त्तुरभावे करणस्य शक्त्यभावात्, "अहं कर्ता" "अहं भोक्ता" इत्याद्यनुभावाच्च, बुद्धिरात्मेति वदति ।। १२५ ।।

प्राभाकरतार्किकौ तु "अन्योऽन्तर आत्मा आनन्दमयः" [तैत्ति० २ वल्ली० ५ अनु०] इत्यादिश्रुतेः सुषुप्तौ बुद्ध्यादीनामज्ञाने लयदर्शनात् "अहमज्ञः" अहं ज्ञानी" इत्याद्यनुभवाच्च अज्ञानमात्मेति वदतः ॥ १२६ ॥

भाट्टस्तु "प्रज्ञानघन एवानन्दमयः" [माण्डू० ५ मन्त्रः] इत्यादिश्रुतेः सुषुप्तौ प्रकाशाप्रकाशसद्भावात्, "मामहं न जानामि" इत्याद्यनुभवाच्च, अज्ञानोपहितं चैतन्यमात्मेति वदति ॥ १२७ ॥

अपरो बौद्धः "असदेवेदमग्र आसीत्" [छान्दो० ६ अध्या० २ खण्ड० १ मन्त्रः] इत्यादि-श्रुतेः सुषुप्तौ सर्वाभावादहं सुषुप्तौ नासमिति उत्थितस्य स्वाभावपरामर्शविषयानुभवाच्च, शून्यमात्मेति वदति ॥ १२८ ॥

एतेषां पुत्रादीनां शून्यपर्य्यन्तानामनात्मत्वमुच्यते। एतैरतिप्राकृतादिवादिभिरुक्तेषु श्रुतियुक्त्यनुभावाभासेषु पूर्वपूर्वोक्तश्रुतियुक्त्यनुभवाभासानामुत्तरोत्तरश्रुतियुक्त्यनुभवाभासैरात्मत्वबाधदर्शनात्, पुत्रादीनामनात्मत्वं स्पष्टमेवेति ॥ १२९ ॥

किञ्च, प्रत्यगस्थूलो अचक्षुः अप्राणो अमना अकर्ता चैतन्यं चिन्मात्र सदित्यादिप्रबलश्रुतिविरोधात् अस्य पुत्रादिशून्यपर्य्यन्तस्य जड़स्य चैतन्यभास्यत्वेन घटादिवदनित्यत्वात् "अहं ब्रह्म" [बृह० १ अध्या० ४ ब्रा० १० मन्त्रः] इति विद्वदनुभावप्राबल्याच्च तत्तच्छ्रुतियुक्तनुभवाभासानां बाधितत्वादपि पुत्रादिशून्यपर्य्यन्तमखिलमनात्मैव ॥ १३० ॥

अतस्तत्तद्भासकं नित्यशुद्धबुद्धमुक्तसत्यस्वभावं प्रत्यक्चैतन्यमेवात्मवास्त्वतिवेदान्तविद्वदनुभवः ॥ १३१ ॥

एवमध्यारोपः ॥ १३२ ॥

अपवादो नाम—रज्जुविवर्त्तस्य सर्पस्य रज्जुमात्रत्ववत्, वस्तुविवर्त्तस्य अवस्तुनोऽज्ञानादेः प्रपञ्चस्य वस्तुमात्रत्वम्; तदुक्तं,—सतत्त्वतोऽन्यथाप्रथा

विकार इत्युदीरितः। अतत्त्वतोऽन्यथाप्रथा विवर्त्त इत्युदाहृतः ॥" इति ॥ १३३ ॥

तथाहि, एतद्भोगायतनं चतुर्विधसकलस्थूलशरीरजातम्, एतद्भोग्यरूपान्नपानादिकम्, एतदाश्रयभूतभूरादिचतुर्दशभुवनानि, एतदाश्रयभूतं ब्रह्माण्ड चैतत् सर्वमेतेषां कारणरूपं पञ्चीकृतभूतमात्रं भवति ॥ १३४ ॥

एतानि शब्दादिविषयसहितानि पञ्चीकृतभूतजातानि सूक्ष्मशरीरजातञ्चैतत् सर्वम् एतेषां कारणरूपमपञ्चीकृतभूतमात्रं भवति ॥ १३५ ॥

एतानि सत्त्वादिगुणसहितानि अपञ्चीकृतपञ्चभूतानि उत्पतिव्युत्क्रमेण एतत्कारणभूताज्ञानोपहितचैतन्यमात्रं भवति ॥ १३६ ॥

एतदज्ञानमज्ञानोपहितं चैतन्यं चेश्वरादिकम्, एतदाधारभूतानुपहितचैतन्यरूपं तुरीयं ब्रह्ममात्रं भवति ॥ १३७ ॥

आभ्यामध्यारोपापवादाभ्यां तत्त्वम्पदार्थशोधनमपि सिद्धं भवति। तथा हि, अज्ञानादिसमष्टिः, एतदुपहितं सर्वज्ञत्वादिविशिष्टं चैतन्यम्, एतदनुपहितं चैतन्त्रयं तप्तायःपिण्डवदेकत्वेन अवभासमानं त्वम्पदवाच्यार्थो भवति; एतदुपाध्युपहिताधारभूतमनुपहितं चैतन्यं तत्पदलक्ष्यार्थो भवति ॥ १३८ ॥

अज्ञानादिव्यष्टिः, एतदुपहिताल्पज्ञत्वादिविशिष्टचैतन्यम्, एतदनुपहितं चैतन्यं तप्तायःपिण्डवदेकत्वेन अवभासमानं त्वम्पदवाच्यार्थो भवति; एयदुपाध्युपहिताधारभूतमनुपहितं प्रत्यगानन्दं तुरीयं चैतन्यं त्वम्पदलक्ष्मार्थो भवति ॥ १३९ ॥

अथ महावाक्यार्थो वर्ण्यते।—इदं "तत्त्वमसि" [छान्दो० उप० ६ अध्या० ८ खण्ड० ७ मन्त्रः] वाक्यं सम्बन्धत्रयेण अखण्डार्थबोधकं भवति ॥ १४० ॥

सम्बन्धत्रयं नाम—पदयोः सामानाधिकरण्यं, पदार्थयोर्विशेषणविशेष्यभावः प्रत्यगात्मपदार्थयोः लक्ष्यलक्षणभावश्चेति। तदुक्तं,—"सामानाधिकरण्यञ्च

विशेषणाबशेष्यता। लक्ष्यलक्षणसम्बन्धः पदार्थप्रत्यगात्मनाम् ॥" इति ॥ १४१ ॥

सामानाधिकरण्यसम्बन्धस्तावत् यथा—"सोऽयं देवदत्तः" इत्यस्मिन् वाक्ये तत्कालविशिष्टदेवदत्तवाचकसशब्दस्य एतत्कालविशिष्टदेवदत्तवाचकायंशब्दस्य च एकस्मिन् देवदत्तपिण्डे तात्पर्य्यसम्बन्धः। तथा च तत्त्वमसीति वाक्येऽपि परोक्षत्वादिविशिष्टचैतन्यवाचकतत्पदस्य अपरोक्षत्वादिविशिष्टचैतन्यवाचकत्वम्पदस्य चैकस्मिन् चैतन्ये तात्पर्य्यसम्बन्धः ॥ १४२ ॥

विशेषणविशेष्यभावसम्बन्धस्तु—यथा तत्रैव वाक्ये सशब्दार्थतत्कालविशिष्टदेवदत्तस्य अयं शब्दार्थैतत्कालविशिष्टदेवदत्तस्य चान्योन्यभेदव्यावर्त्तकतया विशेषणविशेष्यभावः। तथाऽत्रापि वाक्ये तत्पदार्थपरोक्षत्वादिविशिष्टचैतन्यस्य त्वम्पदार्थापरोक्षत्वादिविशिष्टचैतन्यस्य चान्योन्यभेदव्यावर्त्तकतया विशेषणविशेष्यभावः ॥ १४३ ॥

लक्ष्यलक्षणभावसम्बन्धस्तु—यथा तत्रैव सशब्दायंशब्दयोस्तदर्थयोर्वा विरुद्धतत्कालैतत्कालविशिष्टत्वपरित्यागेन अविरुद्धदेवदत्तेन सह लक्ष्यलक्षणभावः, तथाऽत्रापि वाक्ये तत्त्वम्पदयोः तदर्थयोर्वा विरुद्धपरोक्षत्वापरोक्षत्वादिविशिष्टत्वपरित्यागेन अविरुद्धचैतन्येन सह लक्ष्यलक्षणभावः। इयमेव भागलक्षणेत्युच्यते ॥ १४४ ॥

अस्मिन् वाक्ये नीलमुत्पलमिति वाक्यवद् वाक्यार्थो न सङ्गच्छते ॥ १४५

तत्र नीलपदार्थनीलगुणस्य उत्पलपदार्थोत्पलद्रव्यस्य च शौक्ल्यपटादिभेदव्यावर्त्तकतयाऽन्यान्यविशेषणविशेष्यभावसंसर्गस्य, अन्यतरविशिष्टस्य अन्यतरस्य वा तदैक्यस्य वाक्यार्थत्वाङ्गीकारे प्रमाणान्तरविरोधाभावात् तद्वाक्यार्थः सङ्गच्छते ॥ १४६ ॥

अत्र तु तत्पदार्थपरोक्षत्वादिविशिष्टचैतन्यस्य त्वम्पदार्थापरोक्षत्वादिविशिष्टचैतन्यस्य चान्योन्यभेदव्यावर्त्तकतया विशेषणविशेष्यभावसंसर्गस्य अन्यतर-

विशिष्टस्य अन्यतरस्य वा तदेकस्य वाक्यार्थत्वाङ्गीकारे प्रत्यक्षादिप्रमाणविरोधात् वाक्यार्थो न संगच्छते। तदुक्तं—"संसर्गो वा विशिष्टो बा वाक्यार्थो नात्र सम्मतः। अखण्डैकरसत्वेन वाक्यार्थो विदुषां मतः ॥" इति [पञ्चदशी ७ परि० ७५ श्लोकः] ॥ १४७ ॥

अत्र "गङ्गायां घोषः प्रतिवसति" इति वाक्यवत् जहल्लक्षणापि न सङ्गच्छते ॥ १४८ ॥

तत्र तु गङ्गाघोषयोराधाराधेयभावलक्षणस्य वाक्यार्थस्य अशेषतो विरुद्धत्वाद्वाक्यार्थमशेषतः परित्यज्य तत्सम्बन्धितीरलक्षणाया युक्तत्वाज्जहल्लक्षणा सङ्गच्छते ॥ १४९ ॥

अत्र तु परोक्षापरोक्षचैतन्यैकत्वलक्षणस्य वाक्यार्थस्य भागमात्रे विरोधाद्भागान्तरमपि परित्यज्यान्यलक्षणाया अयुक्तत्वात् जहल्लक्षणा न सङ्गच्छते ॥ १५० ॥

न च गङ्गापदं स्वार्थपरित्यागेन तीरपदार्थं यथा लक्षयति, तथा तत्पदं त्वम्पदं वा स्वार्थपरित्यागेन तत्पदार्थं त्वम्पदार्थं लक्षयतु, अतः कुतो जहल्लक्षणा न सङ्गच्छते इति वाच्यम् ; तत्र तीरपदाश्रवणेन तदर्थाप्रतीतौ लक्षणया तत्प्रतीत्यपेक्षायामपि तत्त्वम्पदयोः श्रूयमाणत्वेन तदर्थप्रतीतौ लक्षणया पुनः अन्यतरपदेन अन्यतरपदार्थप्रतीत्यपेक्षाभावात् ॥ १५१ ॥

अत्र शोणो धावतीतिवाक्यवदजहल्लक्षणाऽपि न सम्भवति ॥ १५२ ॥

तत्र शोणगुणगमनलक्षणस्य वाक्यार्थस्य विरुद्धत्वात्तदपरित्यागेन तदाश्रयाश्वादिलक्षणया तद्विरोधपरिहारसम्भवात् अजहल्लक्षणा सम्भवति। अत्र तु परोक्षत्वापरोक्षत्वादिविशिष्टचैतन्यैकत्वस्य वाक्यार्थस्य विरुद्धत्वात्तदपरित्यागेन तत्सम्बन्धिना यस्यकस्यचिदर्थस्य लक्षितत्वेऽपि तद्विरोधपरिहारासम्भवादजहल्लक्षणाऽपि न सम्भवत्येव ॥ १५३ ॥

न च तत्पदं त्वम्पदं वा स्वार्थविरुद्धांशपरित्यागेन अंशान्तरसहितं तत्पदार्थं त्वम्तदार्थं वा लक्षयतु, अतः कथं प्रकारान्तरेण भागलक्षणाङ्गीकरणमिति वाच्यम्, एकेन पदेन स्वार्थांशपदार्थान्तरोभयलक्षणाया असम्भवात्, पदान्तरेण तदर्थप्रतीतौ लक्षणया पुनरन्यतरपदार्थप्रतीत्यपेक्षाभावाच्च ॥ १५४ ॥

तस्माद् यथा सोऽयं देवदत्त इति वाक्यं तदर्थो वा तत्कालैतत्कालविशिष्टदेवदत्तलक्षणस्य, वाक्यार्थस्यांशे विरोधात् विरुद्धतत्कालैतत्कालविशिष्टांशं परित्यज्याविरुद्धं देवदत्तांशमात्रं लक्षयति, तथा तत्त्वमसीति वाक्यं तदर्थो वा परोक्षत्वापरोक्षत्वादिविशिष्टचैतन्यैकत्वलक्षणस्य वाक्यार्थस्यांशे विराधाद्विरुद्धपरोक्षत्वापरोक्षत्वविशिष्टांशं परित्यज्य अविरुद्धमखण्डचैतन्यमात्रं लक्षयतीति ॥ १५५ ॥

अथाधुना "अहं ब्रह्मास्मि" [बृह० उप० १ अध्या० ४ ब्रा० १० मन्त्रः] इत्यनुभववाक्यार्थो वर्ण्यते ॥ १५६ ॥

एवमाचार्य्येणाध्यारोपापवादपुरःसरं तत्त्वम्पदार्थौ शाधयित्वा वाक्येनाखण्डार्थेऽवबोधितेऽधिकारिणोऽहं नित्यशुद्धबुद्धमुक्तसत्यस्वमावपरमानन्दानन्ताद्वयं ब्रह्मास्मीत्यखण्डाकाराकारिता चित्तवृत्तिरुदेति ॥ १५७ ॥

सा तु चित्प्रतिविम्बसहिता सती प्रत्यगभिन्नम् अज्ञातं परं ब्रह्म विषयीकृत्य तद्गताज्ञानमेव वाधते, तदा पटकारणतन्तुदाहे पटदाहवत् अखिलकार्य्यकारणेऽज्ञाने बाधिते सति तत्कार्य्यस्याखिलस्य बाधतत्वात् तदन्तर्भूताखण्डाकाराकारिता चित्तवृत्तिरपि बाधिता भवति ॥ १५८ ॥

तत्र प्रतिबिम्बितं चैतन्यमपि यथा दीपप्रभा आदित्यप्रभावभासनासमर्था सती तयाऽभिभूता भवति, तथा स्वयं प्रकाशमानप्रत्यगभिन्नपरब्रह्मावभासनानर्हतया तेनाभिभूतं सत् स्वोपाधिभूताखण्डवृत्तेर्बाधितत्वात् दर्पणाभावे मुखप्रतिविम्बस्य मुखमात्रत्ववत् प्रत्यगभिन्नपरब्रह्ममात्रं भवति ॥ १५९ ॥

एवञ्च सति "मनसैवानुद्रष्टव्यं," [बृह० उप० ४ अध्या० ४ ब्रा०

१९ मन्त्रः] "यन्मनसा न मनुते," [केन० उप० १ खण्ड० ५ मन्त्रः] इत्यनयोः श्रुत्योरविरोधः, वृत्तिव्याप्यत्वाङ्गीकारेण फलव्याप्यत्वप्रतिषेधप्रतिपादनात्। उक्तञ्च—"फलव्याप्यत्वमेवास्य शास्त्रकृद्भिर्निवारितम्" [पञ्चदशी ७ परि० ८९ श्लोकस्य उत्तरार्द्धः] इति ब्रह्मण्यज्ञाननाशाय वृत्तिव्याप्तिरपेक्षिता। स्वयं स्फुरणरूपत्वान्नाभास उपयुज्यते ॥" इति च [तत्रैव ९२ श्लोकः] ॥ १६० ॥

जड़पदार्थाकाराकारितचित्तवृत्तेर्विशेषोऽस्ति। तथाहि, अयं घट इति घटाकारकारितचित्तवृत्तिरज्ञातं घटं विषयीकृत्य तद्गताज्ञाननिरसनपुरःसरं स्वगतचिदाभासेन जड़ं घटमपि भासयति। तदुक्तम्,—बुद्धितत्स्थचिदाभासौ द्वावपि व्याप्नुतो घटम्। तत्राज्ञानं धिया नश्येदाभासेन घटः स्फुरेत् ॥" इति [पञ्चदशी० ७ परि० ९० श्लोकः] ॥ १६१ ॥

यथा दीपप्रभामण्डलमन्धकारगतं घटपटादिकं विषयीकृत्य तद्गतान्धकारनिरसनपुरःसरं स्वप्रभया तदवभासयतीति ॥ १६२ ॥

एवम्भूतस्वस्वरूपचैतन्यसाक्षात्कारपर्य्यन्तं श्रवण-मनन-निदिध्यासन-समाध्यनुष्ठानस्यापेक्षितत्वात् तेऽपि प्रदर्श्यन्ते ॥ १६३ ॥

श्रवणं नाम—षड्विधलिङ्गैरशेषवेदान्तानामद्वितीयवस्तुनि तात्पर्य्यावधारणम् ॥ १६४ ॥

लिङ्गानि तु—उपक्रमोपसंहाराभ्यासापूर्वताफलार्थवादोपपत्त्याख्यानि।

तत्र प्रकरणप्रतिपाद्यस्यार्थस्य तदाद्यन्तयोरुपपादनम्,—उपक्रमोपसंहारौ। यथा छान्दोग्ये षष्ठे अध्याये प्रकरणप्रतिपाद्यस्य आद्वितीयवस्तुनः "एकमेवाद्वितीयम्" [छान्दो० ६ अध्या० २ खण्ड १ मन्त्रः] इत्यादौ "एतदात्म्यमिदं सर्व्वम्" [छान्दो० ६ अध्या० ८ खण्ड० ७ मन्त्रः इत्यन्ते च प्रतिपादनम्।

प्रकरणप्रतिपाद्यस्य वस्तुनः तन्मध्ये पौनःपुन्येन प्रतिपादनम्—

अभ्यासः। यथा तत्रैवाद्वितीयवस्तुनो मध्ये तत्त्वमसीति नवकृत्वः प्रतिपादनम्।

प्रकरणप्रतिपाद्यस्याद्वितीयवस्तुनः प्रमाणान्तरेणाविषयीकरणम्—अपूर्व्वता। यथा तत्रैवाद्वितीयवस्तुनो मानान्तराविषयीकरणम्।

फलन्तु—प्रकरणप्रतिपाद्यस्यात्मज्ञानस्य तदनुष्ठानस्य वा तत्र तत्र श्रूयमाणं प्रयोजनम्। यथा तत्रैव—"आचार्य्यवान् पुरुषो वेद तस्य तावदेव चिरं यावन्न विमोक्ष्येऽथ सम्पत्स्ये" [छान्दो० ६ अध्या० १४ खण्ड० २ मन्त्रः] इति अद्वितीयवस्तुज्ञानस्य तत्प्राप्तिः प्रयोजनं श्रूयते।

प्रकरणप्रतिपाद्यस्य तत्र तत्र प्रशंसनम्—अर्थवादः। यथा तत्रैव—"उत तमादेशमप्राक्ष्यः। येनाश्रुतं श्रुतं भवत्यमतं मतमविज्ञातं विज्ञातम्" [छान्दो० ६ अध्या० १ खण्ड० २।३ मन्त्रौ] इत्यद्वितीयवस्तुप्रशंसनम।

प्रकरणप्रतिपाद्यार्थसाधने तत्र तत्र श्रूयमाना युक्तिः,—उपपत्तिः। यथा तत्र—"यथा सौम्यैकेन मृत्पिण्डेन सर्वं मृन्मयं विज्ञातं स्याद्वाचारम्भणं विकारो नामधेयं मृत्तिकेत्येव सत्यम्" [छान्दो० ६ अध्या० १ खण्ड० ४ मन्त्रः] इत्यादौ अद्वितीयवस्तुसाधने विकारस्य वाचारम्भणमात्रत्वे युक्तिः श्रूयते ॥ १६५ ॥

मननन्तु—श्रुतस्य अद्वितीयवस्तुनो वेदान्तार्थानुगुणयुक्तिभिः अनवरतमनुचिन्तनम् ॥ १६६ ॥

विजातीयदेहादिप्रत्ययरहिताद्वितीयवस्तुसजातीयप्रत्ययप्रवाहः,—निदिध्यासनम् ॥ १६७ ॥

समाधिस्तु द्विविधः,—सविकल्पको निर्विकल्पकश्चेति ॥ १६८ ॥

तत्र सविकल्पको नाम—ज्ञातृज्ञानादिविकल्पलयानपेक्षया अद्वितीयवस्तुनि तदाकाराकारिताया‍श्चित्तवृत्तेरवस्थानम्। तदा मृन्मयगजादिभानेऽपि मृद्भानवत् द्वैतभानेऽप्यद्वैतं वस्तु भासते। तदुक्तमभिनीय. "दृशिस्वरूपं

गगनोपमं परं सकृद्विभातंत्वजमेकमक्षरम् । अलेपकं सर्वंगतं यदद्वयं तदेव चाहं सततं विमुक्तः ॥ ओम् ॥" "दृशिस्तु शुद्धाऽहमविक्रियात्मको न मेऽस्ति कश्चिद्विषयः स्वभावतः।" इत्यादि [उपदेशसाहस्री० १० प्रक० १ श्लोकः २ श्लोकस्य च पूर्वार्द्धः] ॥ १६९ ॥

निर्विकल्पकस्तु — ज्ञातृज्ञानादिविकल्पलयापेक्षया अद्वितीयवस्तुनि तदाकाराकारितायाश्चित्तवृत्तेरतितरामेकीभावेन अवस्थानम् । तदा तु जलाकाराकारित-लवणानवभासेन जलमात्रावभासवदद्वितीयवस्त्वाकाराकारित-चित्तवृत्त्यनवभासेन अद्वितीयवस्तुमात्रमेव अवभासते । ततश्चास्य सुषुप्तेश्च अभेदशङ्का न भवति । उभयत्र वृत्तभाने समानेऽपि तत्सद्भावासद्भावमात्रेण अनयोर्भेदोपपत्तेः ॥ १७० ॥

अस्याङ्गानि—यमनियमासनप्राणायामप्रत्याहारधारणाध्यानसमाधयः ॥१७१

तत्र अहिंसासत्यास्तेयब्रह्मचर्यापरिग्रहाः,—यमाः ॥ १७२ ॥

शौचसन्तोषतपःस्वाध्यायेश्वरप्रणिधानानि—नियमाः ॥ १७३ ॥

करचरणादिसंस्थानविशेषलक्षणानि पद्मस्वस्तिकादीनि — आसनानि ॥१७४॥

रेचकपूरककुम्भकलक्षणाः प्राणनिग्रहोपायाः—प्राणायामाः ॥ १७५ ॥

इन्द्रियाणां स्वस्वविषयेभ्यः प्रत्याहरणं,—प्रत्याहारः॥ १७६ ।

अद्वितीयवस्तुनि अन्तरिन्द्रियधारणं,—धारणा ॥ १७७ ॥

तत्र अद्वितीयवस्तुनि विच्छिद्य विच्छिद्य अन्तरिन्द्रियवृत्तिप्रवाहः-ध्यानम् ॥ १७८ ॥

समाधिस्तु — उक्तः सविकल्पक एव ॥ १७९ ॥

एवमस्याङ्गिनो निर्विकल्पकस्य लयविक्षेपकषायरसास्वादलक्षणाश्चत्वारो विघ्नाः सम्भवन्ति ॥ १८० ॥

लयस्तावत्—अखण्डवस्त्वनवलम्बनेन चित्तवृत्तेर्निद्रा ॥ १८१ ॥

अखण्डवस्त्वनवलम्बनेन चित्तवृत्तेरन्यावलम्बनं—विक्षेपः ॥ १८२ ॥

लयविक्षेपाभावेऽपि चित्तवृत्ते रागादिवासनया स्तब्धीभावात् अखण्डवस्त्वनवलम्बनं—कषायः ॥ १८३ ॥

अखण्डवस्त्वनवलम्बनेनापि चित्तवृत्तेः सविकल्पकानन्दास्वादनं—रसास्वादः; समाध्यारम्भसमये सविकल्पकानन्दास्वादनं वा ॥ १८४ ॥

अनेन विघ्नचतुष्टयन विरहितं चित्तं निर्वातदीप वदच सदखण्डचैतन्य मात्रमवतिष्ठते यदा तदा निर्विकल्पकः समाधिरित्युच्यते। तदुक्तं,– "लये सम्बोधयेत् चित्तं विक्षिप्तं शमयेत् पुनः। सकषायं विजानीयात् शमप्राप्त न चालयेत् ॥ नास्वादयेद्रसं तत्र निःसङ्गः प्रज्ञया भवेत्।" इत्यादि। "यथा दीपो निवातस्थो नेङ्गते सोपमा स्मृता" इति च [भगवद्गीता ६ अध्या० १९ श्लोकः] ॥ १८५ ॥

अथ जीवन्मुक्तलक्षणमुच्यते ॥ १८६ ॥

जीवन्मुक्तोनाम स्वस्वरूपाखण्डब्रह्मज्ञानेन तदज्ञानबाधनद्वारा स्वस्वरूपाखण्डब्रह्मणि साक्षात्कृते सति अज्ञानतत्कार्य्यसञ्चितकर्म्मसंशयविपर्य्ययादीनामपि बाधितत्वादखिलबन्धरहितो ब्रह्मनिष्ठः।—"भिद्यते हृदयग्रन्थिश्छिद्यन्ते सर्व्वे संशयाः। क्षीयन्ते चास्य कर्माणि तस्मिन् दृष्टे परावरे" [मुण्ड० उप० २ मुण्ड० २ खण्ड० ८ मन्त्रः] इत्यादिश्रुतेः ॥ १८७ ॥

अयन्तु व्युत्थानसमये मांसशोणितमूत्रपुरीषादिभाजनेन शरीरेण, आन्ध्यमान्द्यापटुत्वादिभाजनेन इन्द्रियग्रामेण, अशनायापिपासाशोकमोहादिभाजनेन अन्तःकरणेन च तत्तत्पूर्व्वपूर्व्ववासनया क्रियमाणानि कर्म्माणि भुज्यमानानि ज्ञानाविरुद्धानि आरब्धफलानि च पश्यन्नपि बाधितत्वात् परमार्थता न पश्यति। यथा इदमिन्द्रजालमिति ज्ञानवान् तत् इन्द्रजाल पश्यन्नपि परमार्थमिदमिति न पश्यति। "सचक्षुरचक्षुरिव सकर्णोऽकर्ण इव समना अमना इव सप्राणोऽप्राण इव" इत्यादिश्रुतेः। उक्तञ्च —"सुषुप्तवज्जाग्रति यो न पश्यति द्वयञ्च पश्यन्नपि

चाद्वयत्वतः। तथा च कुर्व्वन्नपि निष्क्रियश्च यः स आत्मविन्नान्य इताह निश्चयः ।।" इति [उपदेशसाहस्री १० प्रक० १३ श्लोकः] ।। १८८ ।।

अस्य ज्ञानात् पूर्व्वं विद्यमानानामेव आहारविहारादीनाम् अनुवृत्तिवत् शुभवासनानामेव अनुवृत्तिर्भवति, शुभाशुभयोरौदासीन्यं वा तदुक्तं,—"बुद्धाद्वैतसतत्त्वस्य यथेष्टाचरणं यदि। शुनां तत्त्वदृशाञ्चैव को भेदोऽशुचि-भक्षणे ।।" इति [नैष्क० सिद्धिः ४ । ६२ "ब्रह्मवित्त्वं तथा भुक्त्वा स आत्मज्ञो न चेतरः" इति च । उपदेशसाहस्री १२ प्रक० १३ श्लोकः । ।। १८९ ।

तदानीम् अमानित्वादीनि ज्ञानसाधनानि अद्वेष्टृत्वादयः सद्गुणाश्च अलङ्कार-वदनुवर्त्तन्ते। तदुक्तं,—"उत्पन्नात्मावबोधस्य ह्यद्वेष्टृत्वादयो गुणाः। अयत्नतो भवन्त्यस्य न तु साधनरूपिणः ।।" [नैष्क० सिद्धिः ४।६९] इति ।। १९० ।।

किं बहुना, अयं देहयात्रामात्रार्थमिच्छानिच्छापरेच्छाप्रापितानि सुखदुःख-लक्षणानि आरब्धफलानि अनुभवन्नन्तःकरणाभासादीनाम् अवभासकः सन् तदवसाने प्रत्यगानन्दपरब्रह्मणि प्राणे लीने सति अज्ञानतत्कार्य्यसंस्काराणामपि विनाशात् परमकैवल्यमानन्दैकरसमखिलभेदप्रतिभासरहितमखण्डब्रह्मावतिष्ठते। —"न तस्य प्राणा उत्क्रामन्ति" [बृह० उप० ३ अध्या० ४ ब्रा० ६ मन्त्रः] "अत्रैव समवलीयन्ते" [बृह० उप० ३ अध्या० २ ब्रा० ११ मन्त्रः] "विमुक्तश्च विमुच्यते" [कठ० उप० ५ वल्ली० १ श्लोकः] इत्येवमादिश्रुतेः ।। १९१ ।।

श्रीमत्परमहंसपरिव्राजकाचार्य्यसदानन्दकृत

वेदान्तसारः समाप्तः।